When the Invitations Stopped

Surviving Domestic Violence

Bettie J. Jones

TEACH Services, Inc.
Brushton, New York

PRINTED IN
THE UNITED STATES OF AMERICA

World rights reserved. This book or any portion thereof may not be copied or reproduced in any form or manner whatever, except as provided by law, without the written permission of the publisher, except by a reviewer who may quote brief passages in a review. The author assumes full responsibility for the accuracy of all facts and quotations as cited in this book. This book was written to provide accurate and authoriative information in regard to the subject matter covered. It is sold with the understanding that the publisher is not engaged in giving legal, accounting, medical or other professional advice. If legal advice or other professional expert assistance is required, the reader should seek a competent professional person.

Scripture quotations used in this book are from the Holy Bible, King James Version (KJV). Please note that Bible passages taken out of context can be used to justify domestic violence. This can be very bad for women in relationships where batterers will twist the scripture to justify abusive behavior. Thus, it is essential to put passages in context by reading several passages that come before and that follow a particular scripture. In all your getting, get understanding.

2008   09   10   11   12   ·   5   4   3   2   1

Copyright © 2008 TEACH Services, Inc.
ISBN-13: 978-1-57258-532-4
ISBN-10: 1-57258-532-3
Library of Congress Control Number: 2008902631

Published by

TEACH Services, Inc.
www.TEACHServices.com

TABLE OF CONTENTS

Dedication ....*v*

Foreword .... *vii*

Introduction .... *ix*

Acknowledgements ....*xiii*

Chapter 1   When Love Dies 1

Chapter 2   At First You Cry 9

Chapter 3   What Shall I Do? 13

Chapter 4   He Took Everything I Had 15

Chapter 5   The Grieving Process 19

Chapter 6   Life Goes on (Surviving) 25

Chapter 7   No Condemnation 31

Chapter 8   Did I Try Hard Enough? 35

Chapter 9   Will My Children Hate Me? 39

Chapter 10 Woman Thou Art Loosed (Jakes) 43

Chapter 11 Father, Forgive Him! 47

Chapter 12 When the Invitations Stopped 51

Chapter 13 Rebuilding Self-Esteem 57

Chapter 14 I am Worthy 63

Chapter 15 I Will Never Leave You 69

Chapter 16 My Life Would Change Forever 77

Chapter 17 Now I'm Free 83

Chapter 18 When God Calls You by Name 89

Chapter 19 Reflections 93

Chapter 20 Resources 97

Behold, I stand at the door, and knock: if any man [woman] Hear my voice, and open the door, I will come in To him [her], and will sup with him [her], and he [she] with me (Rev. 3:20).

DEDICATION

To my children:
Eric, Chaundris, Stewart and Ayanna,
Gerard, Christopher and Arynn
whose love and courage lifted me.

FOREWORD

Christian, Jewish, Muslim and other women the world over, whether young, middle aged or in their golden years, struggle with the question of how to handle a violent and abusive situation, what the Lord requires of wives in such situations, and when to get out of these situations. None of the major religions of the western world encourage divorce and neither do I. And I believe in my heart that God sanctions the institution of marriage. It is His desire that husbands and wives should live together in harmony. For He has said in His word, "Therefore shall a man leave his mother and father and shall cleave unto his wife." Cleave, in the biblical sense, means to become one; to adhere loyally or unwaveringly. The love between a husband and a wife should be so tightly knit that no one should be able to put it asunder.

There are times when outside forces (we will call them *forces* even though in many cases they come in the form of another person, or in the form of events and circumstances) come to bear upon the institution of marriage. These forces, propelled by the fiery darts of the "enemy" or the evil one, cause a cleft in the institution. Attentions and affections are diverted and the love dies. The death of love can bring about distrust, dishonesty, betrayal and abuse, resulting in a loss of hope, a loss of self-esteem and a weakening of faith, making it impossible to serve the Creator as He deserves to be served.

Is it God's desire that women remain in such marriages? Can women serve God and lead others to Him when they have no self-confidence or self-esteem? Can such a woman smile at another and bless another when her own heart is torn and broken? God wants for His people peace and joy. It is a merry heart that does good like a medicine. It is only through such a heart that the blessings radiate, and this radiance leads others to desire the same.

I am in no way taking a stand contrary to biblical teachings and Christian doctrine and belief. I am not encouraging anyone to leave their mates. Churches and major religions frown on divorce, yet it happens in churches all across the country. We cannot bury our heads in the sand and pretend that people of faith just do not get divorced.

I am a woman of faith and many reading this book will be people of faith. Some of us grew up in churches and places of worship; some may have had church weddings because we desired the blessings of God on our marriages. When we got married it was forever—until death do us part. The vows were sacred and meaningful, taken before God and witnesses, and we never expected to end up in divorce court. But we have been there and have heard the judge's gavel; heard the pronouncement that seemingly ripped our hearts out and separated us from the one person on this earth whom we loved the most, and in some cases, separated us from God. Now we are trying to pick up the broken pieces of our lives, trying to mend our hearts back together and to renew that relationship with the Father.

May you find peace and comfort in these words, knowing that God will never leave you nor forsake you.

INTRODUCTION

Something went terribly wrong in my life. The sweet red apples turned to sour grapes. As the apples turned for me, they turned for so many other women of faith. It is my hope that through this missive we can come together to gain strength, support, understanding and empathy. We can do that because we have all experienced the same pain. Domestic violence is a subject that is not so comfortable to talk about. Many women, as I did, hide the fact that they are being abused by their husbands or boyfriends because they are either afraid of escalating the violence or they fear the stigma attached. In some situations, the batterer has threatened their lives as well as the lives of their children. Many women have even been killed by aggressive and abusive partners.

The question of why a woman continues to stay in a situation where she is battered and abused is a difficult one to answer because there are many reasons why women stay. Battered women experience a wide range of emotional reactions, including guilt, shame, helplessness, being emotionally dependent, economically dependent, feeling badly about themselves, feeling isolated, and afraid, just to name a few. The woman may feel that she is to blame and will do everything in her power to avoid a confrontation, thinking that she is a failure, and it is her fault that she is beaten. She may have become emotionally dependent on the batterer and her identity is all tied up into his. Because he has given her no sense of control over her own life, she has no expectation of trying to exercise any control. Economic dependence results when the woman has no money of her own and no way of getting any. Some women cannot even accept money from others for fear they will be beaten for having money that the batterer did not give them.

Experts tell us that low self-esteem and helplessness are learned behaviors, resulting from being identified as one's husband's "property," and worth only the value that he places on them. One of the other factors that motivates women to remain in abusive relationships is that they hold to traditional values of husband, wife, children, and that their children will be damaged if they lived in single-parent homes. Of course, religion plays a major role, too. Strong religious convictions prohibit separation and divorce and I am not advocating either in this book.

Batterers aim to isolate their victims from the rest of society. They do not allow their wives to have friends, and do not allow people to visit the home or allow their wives or their children to participate in recreational activities. With the family having little contact with the outside world, the batterer's abuse is kept a secret.

Battered and abused women of faith, you are not alone. Violence occurs to one out of every five women in this country, this includes women in the churches, mosques, synagogues and other places of worship. It is no respecter of person, class, religious affiliation or belief. In every faction of society and in every culture, domestic violence affects women. In some cultures it is not talked about, but it exists. My hope is that women of all cultures and creeds will find this guide helpful. Your stories are real and

Introduction xi

help is available. Moreover, spiritual help is also available.

I have experienced the pain and suffering of abuse and I survived. I write this missive to encourage others and to help others survive, too. I am grateful for the opportunity to provide a ray of hope for someone else. I pray for your peace.

ACKNOWLEDGEMENTS

How do I adequately thank all those who have cared, encouraged and supported me through the writing of this book? I owe much gratitude to those who believed in me, especially my children whom I tried to protect and keep safe, who cried with me and prayed with me and listened to my sorrows.

I must acknowledge Nadine Kaslow who helped me to discover the meaning of abuse, who provided the first opportunity for me to tell my story, and who helped me to rise above the fear. I thank Gail Ellis for her inspiration and loving spirit, and for sticking with me to see this project through.

When I needed sisterly love, Ruth, Mildred and Joann were there to provide it. Thank you. My niece Stephanie read my manuscripts and wrote words of encouragement and strength, and she prayed the most fervent prayers for me during this process.

CHAPTER 1

WHEN LOVE DIES

Therefore shall a man leave his father and mother, and shall cleave unto his wife and they two shall become one flesh (Gen. 2:24).

What happens when love dies? What causes this death? When did the joy turn to mourning? I remember the days leading up to what was to be the happiest day of my life. The bridesmaids' dresses were ready, the bridal gown was hanging on the door having just a few days before come off the sewing machine, the flowers were ordered, and the last counseling session with the pastor was completed. Even the trip to Basel, Switzerland had been arranged and the packing had been done. The four-hour trip to the Swiss Alps from Wiesbaden, Germany would be a breeze, because love filled the snow covered mountainous air.

The train wound its way over the mountains, through the small towns, into and through the valleys and villages, and eventually into the city of Basel. On the train that night, my husband-to-be and his brother/best man, stayed up all night, too excited to sleep. I, alone in my car, wanted to look my best on my wedding day, slept through the night. The cold February air could not penetrate the warmth in my heart and the joy that filled my soul—the kind of joy that takes the place of food or drink; the kind of joy and exhilaration that robs young lovers of sleep; the joy that passes all understanding.

The wedding chapel was filled with family and friends, and even some well wishers. The ceremony was so beautiful. Walking down the aisle on my fa-

2 *When The Invitations Stopped*

ther's arm, I knew that love would last forever; the traditional vows would confirm it. Vows that were very serious and sacred to me were exchanged before the Lord and witnesses, and soon the pronouncement was made—"I now pronounce you husband and wife." My aunt in Atlanta kept a letter for 20 years that I wrote telling her how happy I was.

When I got married, and I'm sure when you did also, it was forever—until death do us part. This was part of the vows that were meaningful, that opened the door to holy matrimony—the union of two people who pledged themselves to each other without ever a thought that this pledge would be broken. I never dreamed that I would be in a divorce court. But I have been there—as have other women of many faiths.

What happens when love dies? What happened between Basel and the Courtroom? What caused the man I loved with every fiber of my being, to stop loving and respecting me? I have continued to explore that question, to try to find the answer to what caused the death of love that once was so dear. Although my cause or causes may be different from yours, nevertheless the love died. So many outside influences come to bear on marriages, especially if both partners are not rooted and grounded in the Lord so that they can have that heart-to-heart and breast-to-breast love for each other. Such a love comes from the Father who gives us the capacity to love, teaches us how to love; and loves us so much that He gave His only Son to redeem us. Without this agape love of the Father, it is difficult, if not impossible to maintain forever the Eros love. I know now what it means to be "unequally yoked." (2 Cor. 6:14) Modern believers may choose the term "compatible," thinking that as long as their minds are connected and they enjoy similar activities and events,

When Love Dies 3

then that's all they need. Sisters of faith, being equally yoked means being of the same spiritual mind, having the same connectedness with God, having the same desire to do His will and the willingness to put Him first in all things, realizing that no decisions should be made without taking it to Him in prayer, and waiting for His guidance. It means sharing the same faith, the same principles, having the same values and the same willingness to submit your will to His will, and then being able to submit to each other. When this equality is absent, trouble waits on the horizon and the marriage is headed for trouble. You are unequally yoked.

Love dies when one or both partners find it difficult to communicate their needs to the other. When the lines of communication are blocked, neither partner can know what the other is feeling, nor can one work out a solution without the trust, thoughts and feelings of the other. In domestic violence situations, the relationship is one-sided and the batterer seeks to be in control and he exercises his power and superior strength to perpetrate physical and emotional abuse on the woman. It may begin with intimidation that might include putting her in fear by using looks, actions, gestures, loud voice, smashing things, or by destroying her property. The victim is not allowed to express any opinion or to react to such behavior for fear of reprisal. The emotional abuse may begin with him putting the woman down or making her feel bad about herself, calling her names and making her think that she is crazy. He plays mind games. Through the use of his male privilege, he makes all of the major decisions and acts like the *"master of the castle"* rather than like a partner. Thus, the lines of communication are blocked.

Love dies when one partner perpetrates violent and aggressive acts against the other, when the

4 *When The Invitations Stopped*

woman is continually battered, bruised, degraded and demeaned; when she is isolated from family and friends and when everything she does is controlled—who she talks to, who she sees and even where she goes. Love dies when the couple cannot go together to the foot of the cross and lay their burdens on the altar of sacrifice. Love dies when the Holy Spirit cannot be invited into the home because tenderness has been replaced by violence. Love dies when arguments are unsettled and at bedtime the couple sleeps not on the marriage bed together, but on separate beds—even in separate rooms (Eph. 4:26, 31-32). Love dies when tears are not dried, when sadness is not comforted, when hurts are not healed. Love dies when harsh words are hurled against the heart as a javelin is hurled for distance in a field event. Love dies when one partner turns to an outsider to fill the void created when the lines of communication have been severed.

God counsels us as women and wives to be submissive to our husbands (Eph. 5:22), and He counsels husbands to love their wives as they love their own bodies—that their bodies belong to their wives and this means their bodies are not to be shared with outsiders (Eph. 5:25). When husbands give love freely, it is easy for the wife to submit and to receive that love. When, however, that love is withheld and directed elsewhere, wherefore is the submission? When the husband is not the priest of the home, or the provider of the family and the wife has to be responsible for the spiritual leadership (that she is sometimes chastised for) and the provision of bread, lest her children won't eat; when she is insulted, intimidated, ridiculed, belittled and demeaned; wherefore is the submission? When the wife is forced to work two jobs

When Love Dies

to support her children and a husband who doesn't work *one*, wherefore is the submission?

Second Thessalonians 2:10 says that if a man does not work, he should not eat. Yet the meals were continually prepared and served without a question about how they got to the table. Woman was made to be a helper to her husband, not to win the bread for him. When she has to win the bread, prepare the bread and then serve the bread, it puts her out of her comfort zone and makes submission difficult.

This inability to submit goes contrary to the Lord's admonishment to us. Because we know that we are not living according to His plan, this causes a separation or a disconnection from Him. My sisters, the Lord did not intend for His children to live this way. He is not happy when we don't serve him. He says to us "...be kind one to another, tenderhearted, forgiving one another, even as God for Christ's sake has forgiven you (Eph. 4:32). The Lord's desire for us is that we are happy and prosperous (3 John: 2), giving thanks in all things, praising him and witnessing to others about His goodness, He wants our hearts to be merry (Prov. 15:13) for a merry heart does good like a medicine. His light shines through us when there is joy in our hearts.

We can walk in love and do all that we are admonished to do and all that we know to do. We can love deeply and hard; we can prepare favorite meals, light candles and strew rose petals, but then the love dies. First, the realization that the helpmeet is no longer willing to **help** or to **meet** festers within and you ask yourself a thousand times what you did wrong, how you can change, how you can get that love back? The thought that you failed consumes you, sagging like a heavy load. The fact is that you did not fail. Understand that it was

6   *When The Invitations Stopped*

not you personally, but the love itself. When the love dies, it is gone. With this death, comes the ghost of despair, especially when your hopes were shattered and shackled. The load of grief and the weight of loneliness, pain and shame sag like a heavy load.

When love died for me, I didn't see it coming. I was blinded by the love that I felt in my heart, by my sincere desire to be married forever and to fulfill my marriage vow. All those people heard me promise in the presence of God to love and to cherish for richer or poorer, in sickness and in health, for better or for worse, until death us do part. How could it die? Why didn't I see it coming? Or, did I see it and know it and just couldn't face it? I tried as hard as I could try, giving all that I could give and some more. I arranged for counseling sessions which I attended alone. I prayed and cried and held on, but it wasn't enough to make the love survive. My joy turned to mourning when I could no longer make it work. My smile turned upside down and the warm glow of love and happiness turned to a scowl.

When domestic violence is present in a situation like this, there is not much that a woman can do to change things. As mentioned earlier, she is isolated from the outside world, her husband has no desire to change his behavior as his control over her gives him power. He makes her feel like she is to blame for his rage, and he hits, slaps, shoves, pushes, chokes, kicks and punches her to keep her in line or to punish her for igniting his anger, thus forcing him to act violently toward her for a problem that is *her problem*. Because he does not recognize or accept that he has a problem, he refuses to get counseling.

When the late nights out turned to all night out; when the basketball games began at 9:00 a.m. and ended at 2:00 a.m., and suddenly the office required all-night work a couple of times a month, I believed it and just knew all of those excuses were true. After all, I was faithful and just could not imagine there may have been someone else in the picture. I trusted and believed, and when the flowers or candy came, or some other small token, or the kiss and make up came, my faith was renewed and my fears were allayed. I smiled again.

What is typical in the cycle of violence and with a batterer is that he knows that he went too far and he tries to make up by saying he is sorry, by begging forgiveness, by giving small gifts with a promise never to commit such acts again. When the gifts and the promises came, I wanted to believe him, I needed to believe him. Therefore I was extremely happy because the gifts and the promises said that he really did love me and that he needed me.

The games got longer and the all-night work sessions became more frequent. The flowers stopped and the make up sessions ceased, and I asked myself if I could have prevented this painful death. My negligees still fit as my weight had not changed. The meals were always prepared daily and waiting— sometimes wasting because they did not get eaten. The house was clean, the laundry was done and all the dress shirts were ironed. Why was there no love or affection?

Was it the result of the pressures of society? Was it the lack of understanding on my part? Men say, "My wife doesn't understand me." Well, if you would talk to me, I would understand. It's the stalking out of the house and clamming up that I cannot understand. Was it the result of being unequally yoked in the first place? Was it the result of financial stress or unful-

8 *When The Invitations Stopped*

filled dreams or broken promises? Was it the result of the availability of other women who entrap married men because they think married men are safe? Was it the result of not giving due benevolence?

When the pattern changed, the violence and threats against me escalated. I remember on an occasion that I prepared a special meal with all of his favorite foods, set the table beautifully with the good crystal and china, put fresh flowers on the table and lit some candles, and created the perfect young lovers' ambience. Then I sat waiting for the special moment. Several hours past dinner time, the door opened with the remarks, *"turn some lights on in here so that I can see. Were you expecting someone else?"* The ambience was ruined and tears soaked my pillow.

There were times when I dressed up in an alluring negligee and invited my husband to bed only to be told to *"put some clothes on before you catch a cold,"* or *"I'll be there as soon as this program ends or as soon as the other team scores."* Bedtime came at 6:00 a.m. when I was rising for the day. That's when I knew that love had died and there was no resurrection!

No matter how heavy the load, remember, the Lord is there with His hands stretched out to meet you, to comfort you and to give you peace. He wants you alive and well—living abundantly. He knows the pain of your suffering and the grief you bear. He knows your sorrow. He has promised in His word to never leave or forsake you. Behold, I am with you always even unto the end of the world (Heb. 13:5). You have only to grasp His hand. Take His yoke upon you, for it is easy and His burden is light.

Now, it's time to deal with the loss. So what do you do?

CHAPTER 2

AT FIRST YOU CRY!

I cried with my whole heart; hear me, O Lord (Ps. 119:145).

In my distress I cried unto the Lord, and he heard me (Ps. 120:1).

Let my cry come near before thee: give me understanding according to thy word (Ps. 119:169).

...And cry some more! You cry for the love that died. You cry for the pain of that death—for the pain that is worse than death. You cry for the emptiness in your heart, for the loneliness that you feel, for the uncertainty of the future and what lies ahead, for a part of you that died with the thud of the judge's gavel. You cry for the pain you see in the eyes of your children when they ask you what is going to happen to their father. You cry for the relatives who ask if you could have hung in there just a little while longer. You cry for the pastor who advised you to go back—that you could not leave your husband even though you were black and blue from bruises inflicted upon you in what was called lovemaking, but you knew it was abuse. You cry for the years you endured the abuse not knowing that it was wrong, yet knowing that it was not right either. You cry for the in-laws whom you love, but won't be able to see again, because that relationship will die also. You cry for your mother, your sister, your cousin, your friend and your co-worker, who might be going through the same thing, yet won't talk about it. You cry for yourself for not having the courage to talk about it!

10 *When The Invitations Stopped*

In the midnight hour when everyone else is fast asleep, the tears come to soak your pillow. When you are sitting at your desk at work, the tears come to soak your paper. While sitting in worship service, the tears come to soak your Bible. Is the Spirit moving you because it is high among the members right now? Or is the sadness overwhelming you? You cry for the Spirit and for the overwhelming sadness. When you think you are on the road to recovery, the flood gates open again with some small reminder—a song, a man wearing a tie just like the tie you gave him; a memory!

The grieving process is arduous. It is unlike any other kind of grief. We'll talk more about that later in another chapter. When someone close dies, you grieve and mourn their demise. You know that their absence is final and absolute, and there is nothing you can do about it. You go to the funeral and say your final goodbye, and you put closure to that relationship. You get on with life. Grieving the loss of a love through divorce is so devastating, yet it is not a final grief. The one you love or loved is still around—in the next town, down the street, across town, in another state, on the same train with you in the morning, comes to visit your children, stalks you, threatens you. Where does it end? It is renewed with each contact or encounter.

For one whole year I cried. During this year I got into counseling. On the first visit, while waiting for the counselor to enter the room and begin the session, I glanced at the bookshelves. I am an avid reader and am curious about the kinds of books people read. So While I am waiting in doctors' offices or visiting someone's home, I case bookshelves. I spotted a book on the shelf with the title in big, bold letters that described what had happened to me: ***Sexual Abuse and Rape by Persons You Love!*** Reading that title, threw me into a fit of rage and contempt. It brought more tears and shock to me to discover that there was a title—a name for what I had not been able to articulate before. The title described in a few words what had happened to me—words that I could not, had not, dared not, articulate. But there the words were, undeniably bold, staring me in the face, forcing me to acknowledge them, if only in my mind. When the counselor arrived, I was sobbing. I could not accept the fact that I had been raped by the man who said he loved me, who fathered my children, whom I loved, and who robbed me of my youth.

Husbands don't rape wives! Do they? They treat them gently, like sweet and delicate flowers; like doves; like apples of gold in pictures of silver (Prov. 25:11). Yet, the man I loved forced himself on me repeatedly, holding me down with the weight of his body after each attack until he gained enough strength to launch again and again and again! With each counseling session, I understood more about it. The more I understood, though, the more painful it was and the more I cried.

After one year, I was so weary of crying and so debilitated by the weight of sorrow, that I terminated my sessions. The healing could not begin as long as I was in the same emotional place. The pain that I was going through had a purpose, and I needed to transform that pain into purpose. Even though it felt like it would be with me forever, I knew it could not last always. It was there to strengthen me so that I could help someone else.

Before the sessions ended, someone asked me if I had become spiritual after the abuse and subsequent divorce. It was the Lord in my life all the time that helped me to make it through. Had I not walked with Him, I don't know where I would be. He gave me the courage and the inspiration to go forward. He was my shepherd ever leading me off the bridge over troubled waters, but beside the still waters (Ps. 23:2). I had cried enough!

Now I'm trying to pick up the broken pieces of my life, trying to mend my heart back together and renew that relationship with the Lord. To renew that relationship, a reconnection has to be made. Time must be spent in prayer, study and meditation on His Word—talking to the Lord as talking to a friend. Sometimes agonizing with the Lord is necessary, pleading with Him, shedding tears—yes, crying some more, not tears of sadness and hurt, but heart wrenching tears that help to cleanse and renew. God is there to help you pick up the broken pieces of your life. It may seem that He is so far away, but He is always there. So dry your eyes and move. I cannot tell you where to move, but you must move, realizing that God did not let you down!

CHAPTER 3

WHAT SHALL I DO

O Lord, thou has searched me, and known me,
Thou knowest my downsitting and mine uprising,
thou understandest my thought afar off (Ps. 139:1, 2).

Cause me to hear thy loving kindness in the morning;
for in thee do I trust; cause me to know the way wherein I should
walk; for I lift up my soul unto thee (Ps. 143:8).

What shall I do? I am afraid, ashamed, pitiful and downtrodden. I know only pain and suffering. I continue reliving the hurt and degradation, soaking up Kleenex with my tears and finding no peace. Now that my life has changed, I have grieved and cried, friends have forsaken me and I don't know which way to turn. I have pondered the question, what shall I do? I have explored the question as much or as far and I have been brave enough to explore, and for a time I did not know what to do.

How I need to heal! It was only when I made a decision to get better, that in order to do that, I had to stop reliving the past and accept the fact that I was a single woman—like it or not, and I had to move from the place I had spent a year of my life. It was time to dry up the tears and put away the Kleenex.

I asked again, what shall I do? How do I move forward? And you may continue to ask the same question. I had to dry my tears, pick up the pieces and face each new day as it came. I could not plan too far ahead because it was very difficult just getting through each day. At the end of the day, though, I

14 *When The Invitations Stopped*

could look back and see how I made it through. Each day brought its challenges and each situation brought its tests and trials, and it will do the same for you.

When the Children of Israel were surrounded by Pharaoh at their backs and the Red Sea ahead, and with no where else to go, they asked Moses, "What shall we do?" As Pharaoh and his army gained ground on the throng of newly freed captives, they, too, did not know what to do. Moses prayed, lifted up his staff toward heaven and proclaimed, "Stand still and watch the salvation of the Lord." Just as the Lord parted the Red Sea and provided a way of escape for the Israelites, He will make a way for you and for me. Do not be hasty, just stand still, put your trust in Him, and wait for Him.

Hold your head up and take in a new stride. You could move but that might be cost prohibitive. You can paint your house, change the doors and locks, put up some new curtains or buy some new sheets that only you sleep on. I encourage you to accept your new status and get on with life. Take a class; learn how to sew, knit, crochet, paint, garden; surf the internet; make dolls; or create something that expresses your artistic style. The important thing is to do what brings you joy and peace.

See the new woman that you are. The fact that you are now single does not change your personality. Rediscover the real you. You can no longer live as an extension of someone else—Mrs. Somebody. Rather, revisit all those plans you put on hold after you got married. If they make sense to you now, then set a goal to accomplish them. Write an email or personal note to your friends and family. Throw a party and serve good food. Volunteer at the school nearest you or at the local hospital. You might meet some new friends. Forget the fact that he took everything you had. You can get some more "stuff," and you **can** rebuild your life.

CHAPTER 4

HE TOOK EVERYTHING I HAD

*But what things were gain to me, those I counted loss for Christ.
Yea doubtless, and I count all things but loss for the excellency
of the knowledge of Christ Jesus my Lord; for whom I have
suffered the loss of all things...(Phil. 3:7,8).*

The house, the car, the big screen TV, the computer, the furniture, the money in the bank are nothing to lose compared to the loss of dignity, self-esteem, sense of self-worth and confidence that he stripped me of. Some may even have had their children taken away. I had a pastor once who referred to all of those tangible things as "stuff." His philosophy was "you can always get some more stuff," but a broken heart is slow to mend and heal. It's hard to face the congregation you love when you've been stripped of your dignity and left to feel like no one in the world cares whether you live or die. In fact, it has been pounded into your head and buried so deep in your conscious that somehow you believe that you're worthless. Your future seems bleak and you believe you can no longer hold your head up.

How well I remember such degrading remarks as "You're stupid, you're weird, you have no taste. You think you're smart, but you're not; people don't like you." Any negative comment from anyone would confirm for me all those demeaning things and I would replay the tape in my head, reminding me of what he took from me.

There were times when I had to beg for food for my children. I remember once asking my uncle if

15

he would feed my children and telling him that he didn't have to worry about me. One day after church a kind sister shook hands with me and placed a $50 bill in my hand. Others helped by sending me anonymous checks and money orders or dropping off boxes of food at the front door. My pride and dignity were gone. I couldn't adequately support my children and take care of the household expenses. I was totally dependent upon the Lord. When I gave it all to Him, He made a way for me.

It was through my faith and my prayers that the Lord touched the hearts of family and friends who helped me to survive. The Lord was a very present help to me in my time of trouble (Ps. 46:1). "Thou hast turned for me my mourning into dancing: thou has put off my sackcloth, and girded me with gladness" (Ps. 30:11).

I continue taking steps to recover. My joining a book club opened up avenues for me to meet other people, to discuss my feelings, and to give my point of view on subject matters. The intellectual stimulation and exchange of ideas was great for helping me to regain confidence in myself and to realize that I am not stupid as had been pounded into me for so long that I actually believed it.

A change in job gave me a fresh new look on life and exposure to a different environment. Not only did the Lord put off my sackcloth and remove my ashes, but he also clothed me in a robe of peace, happiness and determination. Ever since graduating from high school, I wanted to have a college degree. When I got married, the plan was for me to work and send my husband to school. Once he graduated, he would work and send me. My end of the bargain was upheld and I worked two jobs so that he could complete his degree, but there was never a right time for me. He deprived me of a college education and a more lucrative livelihood. New goals were set: by the time my first child was born; by the time he was 6 years of age and went to first grade; by the time he graduated high school. Even though I didn't reach those goals because the time was never right, once I was free, I re-enrolled in college, completed a Bachelor's degree by going to school at night and working full time while raising two children. I had to overcome some hurdles and travel some rocky roads, but my daughter and I graduated together—she from high school and I from college. By the grace of God, I accomplished my goals.

When the yoke of despair was removed from my neck and I took on the yoke of Christ, He eased my burden, for He said "Take my yoke upon you and learn of me; ...or my yoke is easy and my burden is light (Mat. 11:28-30). The Lord provided a way for me to not only complete my bachelor's degree in three years, but He also enabled me to complete a Master's degree as well, all within six years, including taking one year off to rest.

In Greek mythology, there is a bird called a phoenix. This bird is burned in a pyre and once consumed, rises from its ashes to newness of life. Having been in the depths of despair and having felt all consumed by the violence in my life, with everything I had being taken from me, I, too, have risen from the ashes. The Lord did not let me down. He picked me up from the depths of despair, repaired my broken heart, restored my self-esteem, and placed in my heart the compassion and the desire to help someone else. That means that no matter what was taken from us by those who aimed to hurt us, the Lord will sustain us. The cattle on a thousand hills belong to Him. Not only will He supply our needs, He will also supply some of the things that we want as well.

A smaller television will broadcast the same programs; the house actually looks better without so much furniture, you can find things in the kitchen now that it's no so cluttered, and you needed another car anyway. As long as you are healthy and able to work, you can get some more "stuff!" Just be careful that you don't accumulate another house full of "stuff" again. More is not always better! Whatever he took can either be rebuilt or replaced.

Let us not lament our losses, but begin to rebuild and to stand on the promises. You may have lived in a situation where you were not free to attend your church or place of worship regularly, or to pray openly in your home, or to read religious literature and books. I remember so vividly the threats that if I went to church on a particular day, when I returned home my clothes would be outside; or if I took the children to church what would happen to me; or that the children needed friends other than "church friends." If you experienced anything like this, rejoice and be exceedingly glad. The material things taken from you opened the door of opportunity for you to renew your relationship with the Savior! My prayer is that my testimony will lift the cloud from some other person who is going through something similar. I press toward the mark for the prize of the high calling! You press, too!

CHAPTER 5

THE GRIEVING PROCESS

To every thing there is a season,
and a time to every purpose under the heaven;
A time to weep, and a time to laugh;
a time to mourn, and a time to dance... (Eccles. 3:1, 4).

...for I will turn their mourning into joy, and will comfort them,
and make them rejoice from their sorrow (Jer. 31:13).

Grief is a natural, emotional reaction or response to a major loss, such as divorce or the death of a loved one. When someone dies you know that it is final, that even though that person is gone, their love for you was always there. You may have spent their final days supporting and comforting them. You go to the funeral or memorial service, say your final goodbyes and remember your loved one in a comforting way. However, the pain of divorce is a pain that is worse than death, and just as one grieves the loss of a loved one, when divorce occurs it brings what seems like unending grieving as well.

The fact that someone you love and have spent so much time with does not love you anymore is shocking. Even though you might see signs, you probably think that you can work things out, and may, in fact, be trying to work them out. When you are served papers by a law enforcement official or when you get that document in the mail, yes, you are shocked. You are in a state of disbelief and you ask yourself why? What did I do? What went wrong? How could I have prevented this pain that is worse than death? If you

19

20 *When The Invitations Stopped*

did not want the divorce in the first place, and you tried everything to hold the marriage together, the grief seems magnified. In some ways, divorce can be much more devastating than losing someone through death. The deceased person is no longer around. They are not with someone else, they have not left you for someone younger, they have not had enough of living with you; they are dead. A divorced spouse is around the corner, in the next town, on your train, on your bus, at the kids' school, at the play—wherever you are, you see him.

Grieving is generally easy to recognize, with both physical and emotional symptoms. Some women are often sad and may sigh, sob, cry or yearn for the lost love. While one may miss a deceased person and regret the loss of a love, the pain will eventually lessen.

The grieving process may occur in several stages:

- Shock and denial
- Anger
- Sadness or Depression
- Acceptance

Early stages may involve numbness or denial of the loss. In the shock stage, there may be some confusion and even some disbelief. It is a natural response in a major loss, such as divorce, to deny that the loss has occurred. Some may not be able, or may refuse to grasp the truth of the loss. Some may even experience a deep longing for the departed spouse. However, when the actuality of the loss sets in, the grieving person may be confused and unable to comprehend how or why it happened. After all, you loved him and you tried hard to make your marriage work. You were faithful and you valued the vows; you practiced all

The Grieving Process 21

that you learned in counseling. You may even think that once he comes to his senses, he will come back and things will be as they were in the early days of the marriage. After you wait and watch, you realize that he is not coming back.

Once the realization that he is not coming back and he may even be involved with someone else, some people may enter into the second stage called anger. You are angry because of the pain, the embarrassment, the humiliation, the financial situation you suddenly find yourself in. You are angry because he robbed your children of a father in the household. You are angry because you are now alone and faced with a different set of responsibilities and challenges that you might not be prepared to handle. You are angry because now you must make adjustments to everything. You are angry because he took the best years of your life and now he is enjoying his years possibly with someone else. You are angry at yourself for allowing the loss to occur. You are angry because....

Although it is not listed as a separate stage of grieving, guilt may be combined with the anger. You may feel that you failed and did not do everything possible to prevent the divorce. You may feel like it is all your fault or that it is something you did that caused your spouse to wander and seek affection in the arms of another. You may ask yourself if you were too busy with the children, or with work, or with church to fulfill the needs of your husband or your duties as a wife. You may even feel like you let the Lord down. This guilt leads to a reduction in feelings of self-worth and a decline in self-esteem. You must know two things. One, if you gave it all that you could give it and you did all that you could possibly do, it was not your fault. Two, you must know that with God, all things are possible and you can and will overcome the grief and pain, that you can rebuild your self-esteem. We will talk more about this in another chapter.

The third stage of grieving is **sadness.** In this stage, you may cry or sob bitterly, even at times when you least expect to. In Chapter Two we talked about the crying and all the things you cry for. Your mood may be somber and you may experience deep sorrow or regret. For a long time I had a lump in my throat that prevented me from eating and sometimes from sleeping. When others spoke to me about my well-being, the tears would overflow. In time, my lump dissolved and yours will, too.

The final stage of the grieving process is **acceptance.** In time, the anger diminishes and the sadness eases. You come to grips with the divorce and realize that you must get on with your life. Whatever changes need to be made, you must make them. It is a new day with many new challenges. You can meet these challenges if you face them one at a time, prayerfully and thoughtfully.

Be mindful that grief is a healthy response, and when a loss occurs it is normal and natural to grieve. The stages of grief are not, however, linear, and you may grieve differently at different stages. It is a personal process, often affected by culture and family. Some may express their sorrow openly while others may prefer privacy. However you express it, be aware that is it healthy to grieve because grieving begins the emotional healing. What is unhealthy is to avoid grief or to deny a major life change such as divorce for a long period of time. Such avoidance could lead to serious emotional problems later in life. I am not qualified to address that issue, so I will leave that to the experts.

The Grieving Process 23

The most important aspect of grieving is learning to cope with the loss. Exercise your faith here. Find strength and comfort in knowing that the Lord is your Shepherd and He leads you beside the tranquil, still waters, that He will never leave you nor forsake you. In Him you will find peace and rest, and strength for each new day.

Some helpful mechanisms for coping with grief include:

- Avoiding isolation. Talk to others and explain how you are feeling. Do not be afraid to ask for support. Even though others may pull away from you, seek support from family and other sources.
- Taking care of your physical health. Be sure to eat properly, exercise regularly and get plenty of rest.
- Postponing making major decisions when possible. Grief may interfere with judgment at this time.
- Allowing others to help with those things that are not too personal such as running errands or completing household chores.
- Maintaining a spiritual connection.

Blessed are they that mourn, for they shall be comforted (Matt. 5:4). This comfort allows and propels you into the realization that life goes on.

CHAPTER 6

LIFE GOES ON

This is my comfort in my affliction;
for thy word hath quickened me (Ps. 119:50).

Yesterday I was Mrs. Somebody. Yesterday I had money in the bank, my mortgage was paid, and there was food on my table and in my cupboards and refrigerator. Yesterday I didn't have to be concerned about tuition, health insurance, and car notes. Yesterday I was debt-free. Yesterday I had nice clothes to wear with shoes to match each colored outfit. Yesterday I belonged to that elite group of "married" women, who could talk about their husbands with adoration, admiration and respect; who could laugh about the fun they had last weekend. Yesterday I defined myself by the man I was attached to—joined at the hip with. Yesterday I was in love.

Yesterday I could pay my bills and take a trip to the supermarket on other than my regular shopping day. Yesterday I could drink Tropicana Premium and eat Blue Bell ice cream and Godiva chocolate. Yesterday I could get a manicure and a pedicure and have my hair styled. Yesterday I could meet with my book club and invite people over for social gatherings. Yesterday... the song writer says "it is so hard to say goodbye to yesterday."

Yesterday is gone and the morning has come. Today is a new day and life goes on. I cannot keep living for yesterday. How? What am I to do? I keep thinking of how it was—how it used to be. I think of how much and how deeply I loved and cared. I think of how hard I tried, how much time I invested, how many sacrifices I made. I keep thinking of the long, sleepless nights, the tears, the fears and the need for acceptance. Now I must move forward because the end of something wonderful does not bring the end of life. The death of love is really the beginning of a new you.

Life goes on—perhaps redefined, reoriented and redirected. The road so often traveled may need to be abandoned and a new route discovered. A detour may need to be made. Yes, detours can be frightening because the new road is unfamiliar to you and you don't know where the bumps and the potholes are; the sharp turns and the S-curves catch you by surprise. But in order to get to your destination, you must travel in a new direction. In life, when circumstances change, we, too, must travel in a new direction. The old familiar route has been altered and all of the road signs have been changed.

You know how it is when the traffic is backed up on your way to work. You take another route to avoid being stuck for hours waiting for the road to clear. It is the same with life after love dies. Your way of life takes on a new and different path. It is a path that you have not explored before, but one that you must trod until you get back on the highway—back to a normal life. You cannot sit stuck. You can no longer define yourself by someone else or describe yourself as Mrs. John, Robert, Mark, Enrique, Hector, Abdul, or Steven Somebody; rather, you are now Amy, Mary, Janet, Veronica or whatever your first name is. Look at it as a detour. Even though you are on an unfamiliar road, this new road will eventually lead you back to the main highway—back to a normal life.

Life Goes On

Just as you concentrate on the detour roads, you will need to refocus your thinking and recharge your energies into positive thinking. I had to rid myself of negative thoughts and begin to make plans to accomplish some of my life-long goals. Guess what? He was not sitting around moping and lamenting. My first course of action was to start exercising—something I could do at no cost. It does not cost a cent to walk around the block or around the track in the park or at the local high school. So I headed for the track walking one day a week in the beginning, and gradually walking my way up to four days per week. In time I became a mall walker and discovered the benefits involved. It is a great way to exercise and a perfect way to help you shed unwanted pounds and build up your endurance. Walking also helped to clear my mind. Not only did I clear my head and get in shape, I also made some new friends.

Speaking of friends, prior to my divorce, I had to categorize my friends—some work friends; some church friends, and some telephone friends, because this is the context in which I saw, related to or communicated with these friends. I saw my work friends at work, my church friends at church, and talked to my telephone friends on the telephone when I was home alone. If they called when he was at home, we could not talk. They immediately hung up, or if I was on the phone *too long*, the phone was taken away. Now I had some walking friends whom I saw on the walking track or in the mall. None of my friends, however, could come home with me. I remember once inviting some people home after church. As I was preparing to put the food on the table, my beloved kept demanding my attention—"I can't find my brown

28 *When The Invitations Stopped*

socks; I can't wait for the food to warm, make me a sandwich now; where is my blue shirt?" Every five minutes presented a new request. The people were so uncomfortable that they left without eating. I was so embarrassed!

Now my friends are simply my friends. We can laugh and talk, play and cry, pray and visit, and go out and do whatever we want to do whenever we want to do it. The days of moping are over and a new chapter has opened. I have a new outlook on life. Before I was delivered from the horrific life of abuse and degradation, my prayer for a long time had been for strength to endure, for wisdom to change myself into what my husband wanted me to be. When I recognized that no amount of changing on my part was going to fix the problem, my prayer became, "Lord, please deliver me from what is surely going to be my death if I stay here." Eventually, that prayer changed to, "Lord, please grant me one day of freedom—freedom from the pain; freedom from the broken heart; freedom from the blows and the degrading insults. Just one day—If I live just one day afterwards, let that day be a day of freedom from bondage. I know now how the Israelites felt being captives in Egypt with no way of escape. God heard my plea and in His time He delivered me, and has blessed me with many more days so that now I can bless someone else.

Life does go on. It was not easy. I slept on the floor for three months after moving back into my home because I had no bed and no money to buy one. I recalled the words of the pastor who said that if I lived long enough and was in good health, I could get some more "stuff." Well, the blessings came. Oh what blessings! When I went to the mailbox one day there was an anonymous money order for $100.00.

Life Goes On

Other checks and gifts came just when I needed them most. Some days I would come home from work and find boxes of groceries waiting on my front porch. It's that trust and relationship that you must establish and build with God. He won't let you down.

I got a bed and eventually got some more furniture to fill the empty rooms created when the furniture had to be divided. I celebrated by buying a white sofa. **BOLD!**

My friends can now come to visit. I can have a party if I want to, and I can freely reach out to others. Yes, life does go on, and now I am free!

CHAPTER 7

NO CONDEMNATION

Judge me, O Lord; for I have walked in mine integrity: I have trusted also in the Lord... (Ps. 26:1).

Judge not, that ye be not judged. For with what judgment ye judge, ye shall be judged: and with what measure ye mete, it shall be measured to you again (Matt. 7:1, 2).

It is the finite nature of humans to judge and condemn because they see situations from the outside—through a glass darkly. They don't see the punches, the kicks and the slaps. They don't see the scars and bruises hidden beneath the layers of clothing that hide the beauty that enshrouds you in public. They don't see the scars on the heart, covered by the chest wall. What they see is the façade that is displayed like the beautiful house front that has no floors or plumbing inside, but looks wonderful to the eye of the passerby. They see the charade you play at church or in your place of worship, and in public where you are forced to pretend that everything is okay and the marriage is perfect. They don't hear the threats that if you tell, your life and the lives of your children will be taken, or the children will be taken away from you and you will be declared an unfit mother because he will convince the judge that you are. They don't know that he will allow the children to go hungry and unfed until 10:00 p.m., when you finally get home from pursuing that degree that there was never the right time for you to get, even though you worked to send him to school so that he could get his. He knew that would cause you pain and he could use that against you. They don't see the many nights you sat alone wondering where he was and when he was coming home. They don't feel the rejection that you feel and the repulsion he displays at your slightest touch. They don't know all the intimidation and humiliation that has been perpetrated upon you so often that even you have come to believe that what he says is true. So you condemn yourself.

Then, when it is all over, the sisters condemn you and ostracize you. They cut you off and shy away from you. Is it because they don't know what to do or say that they don't do anything at all? Is it that there are sentinels who want to keep the place of worship pure and feel that the house of worship has no place for you? So they condemn you who never wanted the divorce but were powerless to prevent it. You suffer and bear your grief and pain and shame alone.

I want you to know that God has a place for you and He cares about you. He tells us to cast our cares on Him for He cares (I Peter 5:7). It is in Him that we find justification and salvation. In Him we are free from the shackles that have held us captive for so long. The tears and pain must flee because God now has your back, and He does not condemn.

Remember the woman who was caught in adultery and was brought to Jesus by an angry mob that had already condemned her to death according to the custom of that day? They were ready to stone her to death so that she wouldn't defile the community, much like the sentinels of today who stand ready to dis-fellowship or ex-communicate anyone who does not keep the worship place pure. Jesus wrote on the ground as if He didn't hear them, but they insisted on pressing their case. The sentinels keep bringing

No Condemnation   33

you up before the Board of Trustees, or the Church Board or whatever that body is that governs and metes out punishment. When the sins of the mob were pointed out to them by Jesus writing in the sand, they could not, being of sinful natures, stand in the presence of the Holy One, especially since some of them may even have been with the woman themselves—they dropped their stones and walked away. I don't know what He wrote, but I imagine whatever it was, the accusers read their own condemnation there written in the grains of sand. Then Jesus, seeing no condemning, angry mob but only a pile of stones, asked the woman where her accusers were. "Has no one condemned you?" When she answered, "No one, Lord," He said "Neither do I condemn you..." (John 8:3-11). When the sins of the sentinels come to light, they, too, will no longer condemn.

He wants to save all who will accept Him. Others may condemn because they see only from the outside. In their efforts to maintain purity and perhaps because they just do not know what else to do, they condemn the suffering sisters. Just remember, there is, therefore, no condemnation to those who are in Christ Jesus.

Importantly, ladies, we must stop condemning ourselves. We worked hard, we tried hard, we loved hard, and we sacrificed and made do. We upheld the standards, bore the children, raised the children (raised some husbands, too). We taught, we fought, we prayed, we cried, took care of aged parents (some not our own), planned funerals, attended funerals, went places we really didn't want to go, and no, we did not see it coming! Now, we are on our own. Remember in the previous chapter we were being redefined. It is time to look in the mirror and see the beautiful woman that you are—inside and out. Roll **_up_** that doormat that he has walked on for the last time, and roll **_out_** the red, blue, purple carpet—I like purple because it is the color of royalty. Stand on it with your bare feet and see how good it feels. Take a few steps at a time. Tap into your resources—they are there, and pull out what you need for the moment, for the hour, for the day! Each day tap again. Surround yourself with positive people and positive things.

Love and support are what we need to help us get back to normal. You've prayed and cried enough; give it all over to Him for His yoke is easy and His burden is light! Forgive yourself and receive God's mercy. Guilt and condemnation will keep you trapped in the past. Receive His mercy and go on with your life. This is a new beginning, so stay in the Lord and keep His word bound up in your heart. He wants to bring you back and to save you. Be of good courage. Wait, I say, on the Lord, for there is therefore now no condemnation to those who are in Christ Jesus... (Rom. 8:1).

CHAPTER 8

DID I TRY HARD ENOUGH

In all labor there is profit... (Prov. 14:23).

I gave it all I could give and some more and that wasn't enough. The harder I loved, the worse I was treated. I kept the children quiet and the dog outside and the cat off the furniture. I nurtured and cared, gave due benevolence even when I was sick and didn't feel like it. I cooked and cleaned, mopped and scrubbed, washed and ironed, shopped and baked, canned and froze, prayed and cried, stood, sat, lay, mourned and moaned, held my tongue—bit my tongue! I papered and painted and raked and bagged. How thankful I am that we didn't have a mule and a plow! I sat up nights with sick children while he slept; I sat up nights with him being sick when I had to go to work the next morning. I made countless trips to the hospital and endured the embarrassment of the having the doctors and hospital staff ask about the substances and hearing the blatant denial. Despite all of this, it wasn't enough.

It wasn't enough to drive in the pouring rain and thunderstorm late at night to another hospital 20 miles away because one hospital refused treatment and admission. It wasn't enough that I traveled the long miles day after day to the hospital half-hour early to perform functions that nurses would have performed had they been allowed (bathing, brushing, combining, dressing). It wasn't enough to prepare a holiday meal for the family when the head of the family chose to have holiday dinner elsewhere. It wasn't

36   *When The Invitations Stopped*

enough to prepare a candle light dinner only to be told to *"Turn on some lights because it's too dark in here."* It wasn't enough to prepare dinner for unexpected guests without any notice. It wasn't enough to ask for and expect flowers sometimes because flowers only wither and die. It wasn't enough to stand with tears streaming down my cheeks and iron 25 dress shirts and still not iron the "right" one. It wasn't enough to make my washer and dryer available to his friends who had to pass several Laundromats to get to my house to use not only my appliances but my detergent and bleach, too!

It wasn't enough when at his urging I got my hair cut and styled because I was *"beginning to look like his mother,"* and he did not even notice that my hair was different. It wasn't enough that I sat in the stylist's chair and cried as I saw my locks scattered about the floor around the chair in which I was sitting. It wasn't enough that I locked, braided, curled, twisted, colored, coifed, extended my hair just to please him. It wasn't enough that my identity was all wrapped in his, such that I did not even know who I was anymore.

It wasn't enough to try to bring the children up in the nurture and admonition of the Lord, because they *"needed more than church friends."* So instead of being taken to church, they were taken to ball games, and fast food places, to the movies and to visit other kids, and wherever else that would direct them from the house of worship.

As far as possible, live peaceably with one another, is what Rom. 12:18 instructs all believers. I have to tell you that it takes some super human and some divine strength to live peaceably in a situation like this. It takes strong faith and prayer. It may be by

Did I Try Hard Enough 37

the faith of the wife that the husband is saved (I Cor. 7:14), or by the faith of the husband that the wife is saved. When that faith is rejected and your faith is cursed; when it is no longer possible and when all hope is gone, and you have tried as hard as you can try and you have given it your all, to the point where your health is suffering, your children's health is suffering, and your children are afraid for you and for themselves, you have tried hard enough!

I had a friend who often said to me that I was not tired enough yet. I kept praying for strength and the Lord kept giving it to me. My sister came to move me three times. Each time, I determined to stay and to try a little harder. After the third time when I still didn't go with her, she, too, resolved that I wasn't tired enough yet! My aunt even asked me if I could just hold on until the younger child graduated high school. This same child had missed three days of school because she was afraid to get out of bed because of the verbal fights and the slamming of doors and banging of walls. How much must a child endure? A mother has to protect her children, especially when she has the power to do so. Twenty-two years, three months and 17 days say I tried hard enough!

Remember the story of Job, a perfect and upright man who feared God and eschewed evil. Job was the greatest of all men of the east. But Job was smitten, stricken, stripped and tempted. He endured much suffering and pain. His friends condemned him and no matter how he argued, he could not convince them that he had done no wrong. His own wife abhorred him and suggested that he curse God and die. She was tired of trying. When Job had suffered enough, had tried hard enough to convince others, God spoke to him out of the whirlwind (Job 38:1) and blessed him even more abundantly than he had blessed him before. One day that still small voice spoke to me. Not in the midst of the storm, not in the whirlwind, but in a moment of what should have been passion but was abuse, He said to me, "Enough is enough. You don't have to take this." That is when I knew that I had tried enough. You, too, will know that when you have given it your all, when you have loved as hard as you can, when you have cried as many tears as you can, when you have begged and pleaded as much as you can, you have tried hard enough.

Now, the major question for me is will my children hate me?

CHAPTER 9

WILL MY CHILD/CHILDREN HATE ME?

Train up a child in the way he should go: and when he is old, he will not depart from it (Prov. 22:6).

This is tough, because children need their father. They need both of their parents. They love their parents and want to see them together. They may sense or know that things are not altogether right. But because you are their parents, they expect you to fix things, and they don't understand when you can't fix them.

When the separation came, I took my daughter with me. After a couple of weeks, she demanded to go back home. She missed her father and her room and all of her things. She missed her brother who remained in the home after we left. She missed the family being together, having meals together and doing things that families do.

While driving one day, we passed a church where some homeless people were either sleeping or waiting for food to be served from a soup kitchen. The children asked me if I would take their father back if he became homeless. They could not bear the thought of their dad living on the street and begging for food or waiting in line at a soup kitchen to eat.

Yes, children will hate the idea of the family breaking up and of their dad not being in the home with them. If mommy is the parent who left, they will hate that you left. As they mature and are better able to understand, they will remember waking up in the middle of the night and hearing mommy cry. They will remember the swollen eyes, the black eyes

39

40   *When The Invitations Stopped*

that you explained away. They'll remember the times when the cupboard was bare but mommy produced enough food for yet one more meal. They will remember those times when mommy did not eat, saying she was not hungry just so there would be enough food for them. They will remember sitting in the window waiting all day for the promised trip to the park, to McDonald's, to the circus that daddy never showed up for. They will remember going to bed disappointed and hurt when a promise was not kept. They will remember the missed ball games and the missed school plays and programs that all of the other dads attended but their dad did not. They will remember who sat up with them when they were sick; who welcomed the neighborhood kids, friends and playmates after school, who picked up rocks and leaves, and helped create posters for science projects. They will remember that Mommy said that no matter what, love and respect your father. These memories will help them to overcome the hatred and to replace it with love and admiration.

Yes, they will hate the situation; they will hate the pain and the discomfort; they will hate not having a complete family that lives together, but they will survive. Children are much more resilient than adults. Some will carry the scars and some will bounce back. Your role is to be there for them, guiding them along the way and providing what they need to adjust. It might include professional counseling, or more of your personal attention. Whatever it takes, you must provide it in a gentle and loving way, letting them know that whatever happened has nothing to do with them—that it is not their fault. Remember, it is not your place to try to turn the hearts of the children against the absent spouse. Your job is to teach them to honor their father and their mother as admonished in the Commandments, letting them know that whatever happened between mommy and daddy is between mommy and daddy. Reiterate that it is not their fault. You may be very hurt and very angry, but you must redirect that anger and not use it to poison the minds of your children against the other parent. Listen to their thoughts and provide appropriate answers to their questions that they can understand. Be truthful, but not hurtful. In all things, seek guidance from the Lord in formulating your answers. Reassure them of your love for them. In time, the hate will melt into admiration, love and respect, especially when they see that you are strong because you have been loosed from the yoke of oppression, depression, aggression and degradation. Woman, Thou Art Loosed!

CHAPTER 10

WOMAN THOU ART LOOSED!

JAKES, T.D., 1993, TREASURE HOUSE, SHIPPENSBURG, PA

And behold, there was a woman who had a spirit of infirmity eighteen years, and was bowed together, and could in no wise lift up herself. And when Jesus saw her, He called her to him, and said unto her, Woman, thou art loosed from thine (your) infirmity (Luke 13:11–12).

Jakes, T.D., 1993, Treasure House, Shippensburg, PA. Is there some infirmity in your life that has you bowed together? Are you unable to lift yourself up? As we read the story illustrated in Luke 13, we see that the infirmity afflicting the woman was physical. There are many infirmities today that afflict women—our sisters, our daughters, our mothers, ourselves. Many women in the church and various places of worship today wrestle with emotional traumas brought on by domestic violence and abuse, neglect, divorce, and low self-esteem. These infirmities can be just as challenging as any physical affliction can be (Jakes, 1993).

In my time of deepest despair, a relative gave me a book. Prior to reading it, I felt bound, captive to my thoughts of failure and rejection, to having a dull and ugly countenance. I could not see God's face and was even afraid to enter into His presence lest he reject me as well. I had a spirit of infirmity that bowed me down, and I just could not lift myself up. After reading the book, my soul began to revive.

44   *When The Invitations Stopped*

Whatever the affliction, it is intensely painful, and some of us might feel that we have tried everything that we can possibly try, yet are unable to lift ourselves up. Some situations may even defy will power. In the example of the woman above, the Bible tells us that she "could in no wise lift up herself." Like women today, this woman had probably applied every means of self-ministry that she knew; had no doubt encouraged many others; prayed for many others; but was unable to lift herself up. Many of the women of today go about doing the same—sacrificing so that a child can get a Christian education; rising at 5:00 a.m. to pray for others; accompanying the Disaster van to devastated areas to relieve the suffering of others, but cannot attend to their own situations.

There is, thankfully, a balm in Gilead. God's Word is able to heal and in it you are able to find forgiveness. Jesus said, "Woman, thou art loosed." He did not call her by name. I believe He was not speaking to her alone. I believe that He was speaking to all woman-kind. To her gender, her femininity, the song in her heart that had not been sung; the joy in her soul that had not been expressed; the poem that has not been recited, the music that has not been recorded, the lullaby that has not been sung to a sleepy child, the story that has not been written or told, the laughter and the sunbeam that lights up the countenance, the words that have not been spoken, to the vision in her eye that has not been explored -- to you and to me. He is able to loose us from the infirmities that have us bowed and to set us free to serve Him and to forgive those responsible for the afflictions, so that we can have eternal life.

Turn to Him and allow Him to heal you. God is love, and this love was proven when God gave His

Son for us. John 3:16 tells us, "For God so loved the world, that He gave his only begotten Son, that whosoever believes in Him should not perish, but have everlasting life." Jesus can heal a broken or torn heart. In Luke 4:18 we read that *"The Spirit of the Lord is upon me, because He has anointed me to preach the gospel to the poor; He has sent me to heal the brokenhearted, to preach deliverance to the captives, and recovering of sight to the blind, to set at liberty them that are bruised (abused)."*

Jesus paid the price for you and for me. Allow Him to loose (free) you from the infirmities of the abused and battered life, from the stigma of being divorced, from the ostracism you have experienced, from the loss of self-esteem, from being stripped of your dignity. Allow Him to restore that laughter that is the music of your soul and to give you a merry heart. Let Him brighten up your countenance with a warm, heavenly glow. When you do, you are guaranteed never to be the same broken person again. *"Therefore, if any man (woman) be in Christ, he (she) is a new creature: old things are passed away; behold, all things are become new"* (2 Cor. 5:17). So lift up your head and be exceeding joyful, for great should be your glorying in God! Now you are ready, and you can say with strength and power, "Father, forgive him."

CHAPTER 11

FATHER, FORGIVE HIM

Then came Peter to him and said, Lord, how oft shall my brother sin against me, and I forgive him? Till seven times? Jesus saith unto him, I say not unto thee, Until seven times; but seventy times seven (Matt. 18:21, 22).

...For the pain and the hurt that he caused me. Forgive him for not being a good father to our children. Oh Father, forgive him for the abuse he inflicted on me, for the dignity that he took away from me, for the self-esteem that he robbed me of. Father, forgive him for not loving You. Because he did not love You, he didn't know how to love me. Forgive him for denying me the opportunity to pray openly and for the rejection of your power. Forgive him for the fear he placed in the hearts of my children. Forgive him for not providing for his family, yet enjoying the benefits of being part of a family. Forgive him for the lies and for the ownership he claimed over my life. Forgive him for the nights he stayed out all night long, for forcing me to beg for food to feed my hungry children because he did not provide bread and water. Forgive him for cursing the women of my family whom he knew nothing about—mother, grandmother and others. Father, forgive him for the broken promises and the little hearts that he disappointed. Forgive him for the child support that he refused to pay, causing our children to suffer. Forgive him for the fear and the intimidation instilled in his family; forgive him for the despair and the humiliation he subjected the family to. Forgive him for not setting the right example for his son and for not being the role model that a man child needs. Father, forgive him for the debt that he left me in. Forgive him for the other women that he brought into our home in my absence; forgive him for defiling the marriage bed and for breaking the marriage vows that were so sacred.

The scripture, in Matthew 18:21, 22, provides an example of forgiveness. When Christ was asked how many times should one forgive his brother, seven times? Jesus replied, 70 times seven, indicating as many as necessary—innumerable times. Even in the model prayer, the "Lord's Prayer," we are admonished to forgive others their trespasses before we can seek forgiveness from the Father.

Fellow believers, how can we call ourselves women of faith if we cannot forgive? It is in forgiving that we find peace. Carrying around the hurt, anger and pain creates a dark countenance that can even cause other ills. Pray the prayer of forgiveness and release all of that anger and animosity. When the pain subsided, I talked to the man who perpetrated such evil deeds upon me and told him that I forgave him even though he had not asked for my forgiveness. When you can pray the prayer of forgiveness, my sister, you have arrived and like Jabez, God can and will enlarge your territory and bless you, indeed!

Holding on to hurt and pain keeps you sad and depressed. It is a merry heart that does good like a medicine and a broken spirit that dries the bones (Prov. 17:22). A heart filled with joy can receive added joy just by being open. Darkness lies in the angry, hurt and painful heart. Such pain weighs heavily on an individual, drags the shoulders down and changes the countenance. The darkness and gloom prevent one from reaping the harvest that God has promised.

Father, Forgive Him

That darkness needs to be dispelled so that the light of life can shine through.

Often we of faith pray the Lord's Prayer in rote—blind recitation, without considering the real meaning of the prayer, and the very reverence of the Lord and His being the Patriarch of all mankind. Thus, "Our Father," who dwells in the Most Holy Place (who art in heaven). Hallowed (holy) is His name, whose will it is that mankind is striving to live up to while occupying a space of time on this earth. When we pray "give us this day our daily bread," what we are really saying is Lord, please sustain me for today with all that I need for today, whether it is food, shelter, moral support—whatever it takes to get me through this day. Next comes the plea for forgiveness. Notice the prayer says "forgive us our debts as we forgive...."How does this relate to someone who has taken all you had, including your dignity and your self-esteem? It is not I who owes him anything, rather, it is he who is indebted to me for the best years of my life that he stole from me, for my youth that I sacrificed for his success, for the dignity that he stripped from me, for the bondage in which he held me, for the separation from family and friends, for the separation from church, and for the destruction of the marriage that was so dear to me.

"As we forgive our debtors." Whatever the debt! Remember the parable of the man who owed a sum of money—ten thousand talents. When the servant/debtor was called to repay the debt, he pleaded his case and his intention to pay all of the debt later as he could. He asked the lord to "have patience with me." The lord of the servant had compassion on him and forgave him the debt. Immediately the servant/debtor went out and called in the debt of 100 pence

50   *When The Invitations Stopped*

owed to him by one of his fellow servants. When his debtor could not pay, he had no compassion on him, but seized him by the throat and cast him into prison. When word got back to the lord about the actions and behavior of this servant, the lord called him in, rescinded his pardon and delivered him over to the tormentors until he could pay. . So likewise shall my heavenly Father do also unto you, if you from your hearts forgive not everyone his brother their trespasses (Matt. 18:23-35).

The point here is that in order to be forgiven, we must first forgive. Mark 11:25 teaches that ... when ye stand praying forgive, if ye have ought against any, you must forgive so that your Father also which is in heaven may forgive you your trespasses."

Step out of the darkness of an unforgiving spirit. Let the light of joy and peace into your heart. If the whole body therefore be full of light, having no part dark, the whole shall be full of light, as when the bright shining of a candle doth give thee light (Luke 11:36).

The hurt and the pain made my life dark for way too long. During the full year that I cried and relived that awful pain, there was no light. One day I picked up the phone, dialed the number that had been so hard for me to dial before. Having prayed earnestly before dialing, I was able to say, "I forgive you for what you did to me," not in response to a solution or from the urging of others, but from the depths of my heart; from a desire for light and joy and peace and happiness again; for a renewing of my spirit and the comforting of my soul. It is then that the darkness began to be pierced. It was then that I took steps to change and reconnect, for life goes on. Father, Forgive him!

CHAPTER 12

WHEN THE INVITATIONS STOPPED

*Behold, I stand at the door, and knock: If any man (woman)
hear my voice, and open the door, I will come in to him (her),
and will sup with him (her), and he (she) with me (Rev. 3:20).*

Remember the pre-divorce days when **you** could
choose where you would have dinner after worship?
When you had several invitations and the food was
equally as delicious at either home? Remember how
it feels to remove a steaming hot potato from the
oven or microwave without the aid of an oven mitt?
Just as you hastily dropped that hot potato onto a
plate, your friends, suddenly upon learning of your
new status, dropped you from their guest list. Suddenly, you found yourself making less of a fuss to prepare a meal that you would eat alone. As you eat, you
reflect on the time when the invitations stopped. You
think about all of your "friends" who just don't seem
to have time for you anymore; who are just so busy
that when they settle down in the evening it is past
10:00 p.m. and that is just too late to call; or they say,
I didn't think about inviting you, or we are having a
"couples" party where you won't fit in—maybe the
next party!

So you ask yourself, am I not the same person,
with the same likes and dislikes as I was before the
divorce? Why have my friends ostracized me? Do the
other sisters really think that I want their husbands?
Surely they do not! Why do the sisters intertwine
their arms in their husbands' arms when they see
me approach or walk by?

52 *When The Invitations Stopped*

The invitations stopped because this *is* just that fear in the hearts of many women—that you are now single and may be after their husbands. They are protecting their own. Little do they know that recently divorced women are hurting so badly that the thought of another man is repulsive and far from their minds. We are women of principle, integrity and faith, who are trying to uphold the standards of our Lord, abiding by the Ten Commandments, especially the commandment advising against adultery (Exodus 20:10), and we have no interest in someone else's husband. Many of us have experienced the heartache and pain caused by "the other woman" that caused the demise of our marriages and would not dream of *being* the other woman.

The invitations stopped when I was no longer Mrs. Somebody. The invitations stopped when I no longer had an arm to hold onto or an escort to sit with at the table arranged for couples and not for odd singles. The invitations stopped and we felt the pain.

What we want is the fellowship of friends and fellow believers. We want the compassion and support of our married sisters and of like-minded people of faith. We want and need spiritual support and guidance; someone to talk to, to pray with and to cry with. We need assistance, not condemnation. We want dinner for more than one sometimes, although a table for one can be a refuge. We want the encouragement that propels us into another day. Yet, we find ourselves eating alone. Is it that our friends and fellow believers fear that their invitations will be rejected? Is it their not knowing how to reach out or what to say? Maybe they are afraid you will talk about the situation and they won't know how to react especially if they were friends with the departed spouse. They should not worry because we don't want

When The Invitations Stopped 53

to talk about our failed marriages all the time. Whatever it is, we are the ones left out.

I am reminded of the parable of a certain king who prepared a wedding feast for his son. When it was time for the ceremony, the guest hall was vacant.—Empty. The king sent his servants out to remind the invited guests that it was time for the wedding to start. All of the invited guests had something else to do and could not go in to the feast. The king again sent his servants to invite other guests but they, too, begged off for one reason or another. The third time, the king sent his servants to the less fortunate—the homeless, the indigent, the widowed and the divorced. He even provided them with wedding garments so that no one had to be aware of the social status of another. Thus, the banquet hall was brimming with guests who were all made to feel loved, important, and whose presence was vital to the esteem of the host, the ceremony and the celebration. He needed the guests and no matter their status, they were made welcome and made to feel like they belonged.

As these wedding guests were made to feel special, divorced people also want to feel special. We don't want to be identified as someone who does not fit in anymore. We want to wear the garment of acceptance and the headdress of belonging. We want to don the sash of sisterhood. We have been in similar situations where we have been rejected and dropped from the list because the fit wasn't quite right. Our one paycheck does not stretch as far and we have to wear the same outfit we wore last year—no wedding garment or no party dress.

When the invitations stop and dinner for one is all there is, remember that dinner for one can actually be fun. It just depends on how much you love yourself—you have to get back to that point of loving yourself again! Make your dinner a delight by putting on that fresh linen tablecloth. Add some fresh flowers from your garden or from the florist if you don't have any blooming flowers in your yard, light some scented candles and allow the soft glow and fragrance to create a special atmosphere (aroma therapy). Take out the fine china and the crystal that is beautifying your cabinet and that you are saving for a special occasion. Set yourself an elegant table with the flowers arranged in the center. Then prepare a gourmet meal and enjoy it. This is the special occasion—it is the dawn of the new you. So go ahead and celebrate the new you!

My sister visited me once when I had all of my "good dishes" packed away waiting for my daughter to inherit. She said to me that the china and crystal would not mean anything to my daughter, that she would probably sell them and spend the money frivolously. "Use them; enjoy them yourself. Everyday that you live free of hurt and pain is a special occasion." I took her advice. Now I serve my grape juice or sparkling apple juice in a flute and eat my dessert from the most delicate Mikasa. Try having your griller or fish or whatever your favorite meal is on your best china. See how good it makes you feel. You don't have to sit around waiting for an invitation. Next week, plan your own dinner party and invite someone outside of the circle home for a meal. You might make a new friend or encourage someone's heart.

On the light side, my husband didn't like candles, so the soft glow and scent of sweet vanilla was not present in my home. Now I can not only light candles on the dining table, but I can light them all over the house if I choose.

When The Invitations Stopped   55

Eating alone allows me to play tricks on society. You know, all the rules of etiquette that one must observe when eating in the company of others, like not licking your fingers, and breaking your bread in small pieces and buttering each piece as you eat it. When I eat alone I can lick my fingers if I choose, or not break bread in bite size pieces and butter a whole slice at once. Now you can make your own rules—remove your girdle— that awful tight-fitting garment that holds you in, sometimes so tightly that you can hardly breathe. You hate them anyway, but you wear them because somebody made it a rule. Again, make your own rule; now that you are free, remove your girdle and **_be_** free!

Even though our friends have disassociated themselves from us, we have a Savior who is full of compassion; who gives joy and who quells the loneliness within us. Then He clothes us in His righteousness and He prepares a table before us in the presence of our enemies (Ps. 23)—what a table! He anoints our heads with oil—the sweet oil of the Holy Spirit. Use all of the missed social events as times to draw closer to the Lord. Strengthen your prayer life, study more, get caught up on the reading that you have always wanted to do but never had time. Let this be the year that you read the Bible through—and this time stick with it. Plant a garden or crochet a blanket. Set goals and make plans to accomplish them. Moreover, invite someone to have dinner with you!

Pray for those friends who no longer invite you home; they are missing out on a true friend and great fellowship. Be encouraged, for we have a friend in Jesus who does not condemn and who does not leave us alone. His invitation is always open. He is waiting for your R.S.V.P.

CHAPTER 13

REBUILDING YOUR SELF-ESTEEM

Beloved, I wish above all things that thou mayest prosper and be in health, even as thy soul prospereth (3 John 2).

And be renewed in the Spirit of your mind; And that ye put on the new man (woman), which is after God is created in righteousness and true holiness (Eph. 4:23, 24).

You have been battered so much that you don't know how it feels to be whole and new again. You have been so afraid of holding your head up for fear that your cheek will encounter the open palm of another that the ground is all that you have been seeing lately. You can not seem to remember how it feels to choose the clothes that you want to wear and to wear them proudly. You may even ask how can you rebuild from nothing and where do you find the strength and dignity that has been destroyed? First, realize that with Christ all things are possible. Philippians 4:13 reminds us that "I can do all things through Christ which strengthens me." After you have prayed and cried, for the tears will come—even at moments when you least expect them—then feast on the text and set about rebuilding.

When a builder gets ready to construct a building, there are several things he needs to do. First, he develops a set of plans and then he works from that set of plans to do everything related to getting the building erected and standing tall. Like the builder, you must establish a plan to rebuild your self-esteem. It is time to do some heavy construction!

58 *When The Invitations Stopped*

If necessary, take out a picture of yourself that was taken at a happier time in life. Resolve to look like that again. Remember that you have been declared worthy. Knowing this, embrace that feeling and believe in your heart that you are, indeed, worthy. Start with a self-makeover. Get your hair done—change your hairstyle; get your nails manicured and if you have never had a pedicure, get one. Pamper yourself. Buy that perfume that you have always wanted but thought you could not afford. Then do a makeover in the house. Redecorate. Get rid of those ugly sheets and worn out bedspread or comforter; open the blinds and let the sun shine in. Light some scented candles. Doing this may not be easy and it may take some time to replace some things. After all, he took everything. For the first three months I slept on the floor because he had taken the bed. That was okay because I didn't want that defiled bed anymore anyway.

If there are things in the house that cause you pain, get rid of them. Your heart cannot mend if it is constantly reminded of the hurt. As I mentioned earlier, I was in counseling for one whole year, repeating and reliving the story. Realizing that I could not continue in the same place, and that I needed relief from the suffering, I did a makeover. I not only changed the locks, I changed the doors also, the drapes and the dishes, and everything else that brought me pain. In time, I recovered and so will you. Now I feel good about life.

Now that the house is the way you want it, try getting *out* of that house that has held you captive for so long. Volunteer at a hospital or Nursing Home; do something for someone else, especially someone less fortunate, and discover that you have some-

Rebuilding Your Self-esteem 59

thing to offer. When someone else depends on you for something—a meal, a bath, to have a story read to them, or to have a cut flower placed on their night stand, you must muster up the strength to not let them down.

If you like roller skating but he didn't, so you could never go skating, now is your opportunity to visit the rink. Learn to drive, get a library card, check out some good books and read. You will broaden your vocabulary and meet some new friends. If you always wanted to be a vegetarian but couldn't because you had to keep cooking meat and potatoes for the carnivore in your house, now is the time to do it. Have lunch with a friend or with a group of friends either from your place of worship or from your work place. Get dressed up—take that dress that you have been hiding out of the closet and wear it, or buy a new dress. Take a bubble bath—create your own spa by perfuming your bath and lighting candles all around the tub. Stop eating alone at home! Treat yourself to dinner, then treat a friend or work associate; do something positive each day that you can feel good about. If you have always wanted to go back to school but couldn't do so, enroll in a course or two. If you already have a degree, learn to knit, crochet a lap blanket for an elderly person and take it to them, paint, garden, surf the internet, make dolls or create something that expresses your artistic style, become a gourmet cook; take a computer class; start your own business—be brave.

Having to speak in front of a room full of students and professors helped to rebuild my self-esteem and to restore my dignity. I had a voice and people were interested in what I had to say. It feels good when younger students respect you and consider you wise.

When others value your opinion, it gives you a sense of worthiness. This may not be the answer for you, but the point is for you to engage in activities that will increase your self-esteem and restore your dignity and self-worth. You can do it!

Those were initial steps in rebuilding my self-esteem. A new wardrobe helped, too. It was off with the drab and on with the vibrant. I discovered that I had legs above my ankles that were hidden beneath the ankle-length dresses, and my legs were shapely, too—distinct ankles and calves. No, I didn't get carried away, I followed the principles of modest dress for Christian women. Then came a change in hairstyle. If you have always wanted a different look but were afraid or not allowed to try it, now is your time. Cut, style, braid, twist, lock, whatever suits your fancy. Do it! It will take years off your face and you will feel good about yourself.

Take heart to the words of Solomon: To everything there is a season, a time for every purpose under heaven (Eccl. 3:1). It is your time and your season. Accept the new you and your new status, and get on with life. Look at yourself in the mirror and see the new woman. Now you can be Ms. Somebody—Ms. Betty, Ms. Mary, Ms. Johnson. It's funny how when the designation *Ms.* was first introduced, I hated it. I could not see what group of women it represented. Now, it is not so offensive. Now I'm known in some circles as Ms. Bettie, and I like it.

Remember what you looked like at 19, at 25 or 30, or at whatever age. Remember what you looked like without the swollen eyes and the puffy cheeks, and make a resolve to look like that again. Lose the ten pounds that you put on after the breakup because you sought comfort in food. Besides, your doctor has

Rebuilding Your Self-esteem

suggested that you lose them anyway. Revisit all of those plans that you put on hold after you got married. If they make sense to you now, then set a goal to accomplish them. You can do it!

The point is, in order to rebuild your self-esteem; you must first feel good about yourself. Tell yourself that you are beautiful and you are worthy. Start by loving yourself again. Accept the fact that it is over and stop sitting up all night long and crying yourself to sleep in the wee hours. You are important and your life is meaningful, with a plan and a purpose. When you feel good about yourself, you can then share your gifts and talents with others. You can unlock the door to your full potential, and then develop that potential into what you have always dreamed about. If you have children in school, learn the new math or the new style of teaching children to read and write—to build sentences and paragraphs. You will be amazed at the changes in learning that have occurred over the years. Read a book—read some books so that you can build your vocabulary and become a great conversationalist.

If you have put off exercising because you felt like you had no one to look good for, start again. Look good for yourself. Walk, jog, run, push up, sit up, do whatever is comfortable for you, but get back in shape and then look in the mirror and see the beauty that God created in you.

Remember the makeover? Well, now it is time to donate all of your old clothes to charity and to update your wardrobe. Every woman wants a new dress or suit. See how much better you will feel when you have a new outfit. Change your hairstyle; get some new glasses if you wear glasses. Better yet, get rid of the glasses and get some contacts. Wow! What a difference they make! You have had your pedicure, now show off your pretty feet.

When you feel good about yourself, you feel good about life. When you feel good about life, you feel good about living it to the fullest. God has given your life new meaning and new direction, now you can live the abundant life and know that you are worthy!

CHAPTER 14

I AM WORTHY

Then Jesus answered and said unto her, O woman, great is thy faith: be it unto thee as thou wilt... (Matt. 15:28).

Have you ever felt that because of your shortcomings or because you did not achieve a goal or meet a deadline, you were not worthy... of respect, recognition, or consideration? Did you feel because the man you married could not see your beauty and your strength, and because he misused you and maybe even abused you, that you were the cause and deserved the harsh words and evil deeds perpetrated against you, and were not worthy of anything better?

As women, we must cease taking on the burdens and the weights of others. As one of the Master's children, you are worthy because He proclaims you to be worthy. Prov. 18:22 says that "He who finds a wife, finds a good thing, and obtains favor from the Lord." Who can find a virtuous wife? For her *worth* is far above rubies (Prov. 31:10). The ruby is a beautiful, precious, red stone that Solomon, one of the wisest men who ever lived, compares a woman's worth to. In fact, Solomon declares her worth to be above this gem. So let no man tell you that you are not worthy.

During creation's week, God in His infinite wisdom created woman. He must have been pleased because He brought her and gave her to the man. Woman was blessed by God and therefore worthy of respect, worthy of right treatment and worthy of honor as a wife. So unload the weight you have been carrying. Dry up the tears and stop rehearsing the

64   *When The Invitations Stopped*

awful scenes in your mind. Begin the process of healing your broken heart.

How do you do that? What works for me may not work for another. But for me, the healing began when I said enough is enough! Enough counseling, enough crying, enough sleepless nights, enough yearning for a love that was never going to be mine again. I made a decision that with God's help I was moving out of heartbreak hotel into a luxury condominium. I asked for His help and He guided me all the way.

When the friends stopped calling and the invitations stopped coming, I found a friend in Jesus. The tears dried up and a new door opened. I found that I had more time to devote to studying the word and as I studied, my relationship with the Lord grew stronger. As I grew stronger, I began to rebuild my self-esteem. Heaven knows all of my dignity and self-esteem had been stripped from me through the constant barrages of mean, slanderous, demeaning and degrading insults; through the physical and mental attacks, the put-downs and embarrassments; the false accusations; the withholding of affection and the denial of basic life necessities.

My first venture into esteem building was frightening and I wondered if I could do it. But I purposed in my heart that I was going to complete a college degree. With no money and two children in school, I enrolled. Through grants, loans and the assistance of relatives, I graduated with honors. Praise be to God!

While in school I discovered that I had a voice and others were interested in what I had to say. In a law class, and as a member of a team deciding the fate of an NBA star, my opening and closing statements enabled my team to win. Talk about a boost to my self-worth! I was fascinated with research and joined

I Am Worthy   65

a research team that examined how abuse/domestic violence was linked to attempted suicide in women aged 18 to 64. At a group meeting of medical students and nurses involved in the study, I told my story as I mentioned in a previous chapter. They left that meeting with a different perspective of how to treat women reporting to them with bruises and aches and pains that may be physical or emotional. I had a voice that was heard and an opinion that was valued.

"I wish above all things that you prosper and be in health" (3 John:2). "Being in health" means being in a good physical, mental and spiritual condition. God has already whispered your name and called you to newness of life. He has blessed you and strengthened you to make it through the clouds because He says that you are worthy. Now you must believe that you are worthy.

When I discovered there was a name for what was happening to me, I rejoiced in a sense. Prior to that time I had no way of articulating the fear and the pain. The words to adequately describe my life were not part of my vocabulary. Or, was it the shame I feared if someone actually knew? When a baby discovers that she can make audible sounds, she rejoices in those sounds and the sounds grow louder and the baby becomes more confident in this new found ability. She talks out in church, on the bus, when mommy is on the phone, wherever she happens to be. Like a baby, upon discovering that what I was going through had a name, albeit not a good name, I rejoiced at the revelation! I rejoiced at knowing that I did not deserve the abuse; that it was not my fault, and that I did nothing to cause it. What I learned I wanted to share with others. What I have later learned is that abusers act out of their own fears, shortcomings, oppressions and inadequacies. Knowing myself, I could look at others and know what was going on in their lives, too.

This discovery also helped me to realize and understand that I did not deserve that kind of treatment, that I am a child of the King, worthy of so much more. You don't deserve it and neither does any other woman. Women were created to be help meets, not to be battered and abused; but to be pampered and protected, not to be degraded and belittled; but to be strong and elegant, not to be slumped and cowered into believing that we are less that what God created us to be.

About a year after the demise of my marriage, a relative introduced me to someone I had never heard of before—T.D. Jakes—and his book "Woman, Thou Art Loosed." What an uplifting experience! After reading that book, I knew I had been set free and the wounds of the past began to heal. The victim had begun to survive!

I had worn the yoke far too long. Now it was time to straighten out my slumped shoulders, stand tall with a smile on my face and a glide in my step. It was time to gird myself with the breast plate of righteousness and the shield of faith. It was time to take up the sword and march to a different drummer. It was time to come out of the shadows and the dark crevices and to allow the light of God to illumine me. It was time to recognize that the Father would deliver me and to know that I am worthy of respect! I am worthy of honor! I am worthy of the dignity that had so long ago been taken away! I am worthy and you are worthy because God says that we are. And if He says so, I believe it and I claim it! Once you have that connection with Him and He is ordering your steps,

I Am Worthy

you can sincerely say, with a new attitude and with conviction, I know that You did not let me down. I say again, "Speak Lord, for Thy servant heareths! I am moving forward in His name because I know that He will never leave me.

CHAPTER 15

I WILL NEVER LEAVE YOU:
GOD DIDN'T LET YOU DOWN

Let your conversation be without covetousness; and be content with such as ye have: for he hath said, I will never leave thee, nor forsake thee (Heb. 13:5).

"I will never leave you nor forsake (abandon) you (Heb. 13:5)." This is a promise from the Lord, and His promises are true. Unlike the promises of the wedding vow…"To have and to hold until death us do part." Was this your sacred vow? Was this the vow that was repeated to you in front of God and witnesses? This promise was so sweetly made and yet so bitterly broken.

Marriage is honorable in all, and the bed undefiled (Heb. 13:4). It is when intruders are allowed or invited in that the marriage bed becomes defiled. I met a woman after my divorce who, when introduced to me, said, "Oh, I've been to your house many times when you weren't home." Was my bed defiled? Yes, someone else had been invited, allowed, welcomed, and seduced into an honorable place… a place ordained for a husband and wife; a place where life begins; a place where little ones come in the middle of the night when they are afraid and need to be comforted.

What did that do to me? Another renewing of my pain; another piercing of my heart. How many others? How much more? How many sheets do you burn? Which sheets do you burn? Do you burn the bed?

What happed to the promise? Did I try hard enough? Was it at first the circumstance of being in

69

the same place as someone who made herself available? Was it intentional all the while and became a habit that was difficult to break? What made him cheat? What caused all the qualities that he loved about me to transform into something distasteful? Maybe I gained or lost a few pounds, but I still took care of myself. Was it an invitation to an office party without me, or a business trip out of town that thrust two people together and the attention from someone new who was exciting overwhelming? The snow flake grew into a snowball, and rolled farther and farther down the hill of despair. When it melted, it killed the marriage. You can no longer live in denial and accept the blame as he has tried to transfer it onto you. He is the person who cheated, not you!

You and I have heard the standard answers of "she understands me," yet when you and I have tried to talk, they stormed out of the house. When I wanted to go out he was too tired. When there was a problem, it was my problem that I needed to find a solution to. When I suggested professional help, he didn't need anyone else telling him how to run his marriage. He could handle and resolve his own problems. When you lit the romantic candles it was too dark in the room and he couldn't see. When you prepared the special meal, he was dieting and exercising and could not eat what you prepared.

When the other woman came along, she didn't want to talk or ask questions, or solve problems. She didn't have children to care for, or schedules to juggle, games to go to, or practice to attend or homework to do. She wanted pleasure and she made herself available. The guilt he felt for having engaged himself precipitated violence and abuse when he came home.

I Will Never Leave You: God Didn't Let You Down   71

The children weren't quiet enough; the TV wasn't on the right station; the food wasn't seasoned properly; the **right** shirt was not ironed even though you had stood and ironed 25 shirts with tears streaming down your face. **I will never leave you!** But you're gone already; you left me long before you walked out of the door and said goodbye.

When you reach across the bed at night and your touch is rejected as something extremely repulsive; when he sleeps so close to the opposite edge of the bed that a slight touch would topple him over the edge; when the phone rings late at night and he leaves home; when an invitation for *one* to Thanksgiving dinner is extended and accepted and you are in the kitchen preparing dinner for the family, you know he has left you. When he stays up or out all night, and even though he continues to come home to change clothes and to sleep in the bed once you get out of it, the promise has been broken. When the Victoria Secret lingerie is no longer appealing, you know he has left you long before the final decree. But, you keep hearing "I will never leave you, No matter what..." followed by "You're nothing! You're too skinny; you're weird; you don't know how to dress or fix your hair! You think somebody wants you? Nobody wants you. I'm going to show you what it's going to be like when you're out there on your own (another knee slammed into my thigh; another forceful thrust into my body—slam, pound, thrust! Until I was so weak that I could no longer stand or walk). I'm going to make you remember...

I remember, yes, I remember.... Yolanda Adams sings about remembering, but her remembrance is sweet and good. My remembrance is horrid and sad, degrading, egregious! Yet, the memory invades my soul and my spirit at times when I am unaware, when I'm alone with my thoughts, when I seek solitude and peace from the trials of life. I remember the lonely days and nights; the dinners eaten alone; the dinner times without food so that the children could eat; the begging of food for the children from friends and relatives; the false accusations; the penalty for wanting a new dress; the punishment for not keeping a 2-year old quiet. How can it be done? Tell me how to quiet a two-year old!

I remember the Thanksgiving at home alone with the kids, meal in progress, when he was enjoying the holiday with another family. I remember trying to explain to the kids why daddy wasn't home to have Thanksgiving with them. I remember the missed birthday party but the arrival to take another woman and her children home after the party.

I remember the trip to the hospital on the bus alone. I remember the cold steel bed and the unfriendly faces of obstetric nurses who had delivered thousands of babies and were not sensitive to my pains and need for comfort and reassurance—the sterile green sheets and commands to push and don't push—all alone in a hospital while daddy was at home sleeping.

I remember the near miscarriage; lying in a bed with my head down and my feet elevated, in an extremely cold and dark room, threatening to lose my first born child because of the abuse I suffered. How much do I remember? How much have I forgiven? No matter what I did it was never enough! No matter how hard I tried, I didn't try hard enough! ... What I wore, it wasn't pretty enough! .... How I did my hair, it wasn't stylish enough. Even when I cut it into a style, the style wasn't pleasing enough. No

I Will Never Leave You: God Didn't Let You Down 73

matter what! If I stayed home, or if I went to work, or went to church, or to the supermarket, or made a candlelight dinner or a TV dinner, or an apple pie or a chocolate cake, it wasn't enough!

It wasn't enough to be called at 1:30 a.m. in the dead of winter to drive 60 miles to pick him up because his car wouldn't start, having to wake children to make the journey because they were too young to be left alone sleeping, only to arrive in the freezing cold to find him and another woman stranded, and my having to drive her home! I remember that he didn't get into the front seat with me, but climbed into the back seat with her. The humiliation, the hurt and the pain were devastating. It was drive her home or risk being abused after I got home.

It wasn't enough that he used my car to go to work with a promise to pick me up downtown at 7:30 p.m. I waited and waited and waited, refusing several offers of rides home, because I knew he would be angry if I left prior to his arrival. Yet the last bus left, the last person left as the building closed at 10:00 p.m. and I was still sitting and waiting, alone and afraid in downtown Atlanta. When he did arrive at 10:20 p.m., there was someone else in the car that needed to be taken home. I Will Never Leave You!

I forgave and forgave and forgave, yet I remember that no matter what... I still loved deeply and wanted to be loved in return. But the love was not returned, rather, it was given to someone else. How many others? I don't know. What I do know is that there were parties going on at my house while I was at work and the messes were left for me to clean up. I know the heartache and pain of sharing my husband with someone else who knew all about me but I knew nothing about her. I know the suffering of abuse, the

74 *When The Invitations Stopped*

pleas for forgiveness and the promises to do better. I know the insults and the degrading remarks that seemed so easy to roll off the tongue. I can hear the words ringing in my ear, "You're stupid, you need me to make it and I'm not helping you."

Through it all, know that God did not let you down. My sisters, remember that "No matter what...." God says "I will never leave you nor forsake you. Lo, I am with you always, even to the end of the world (Matt. 28:20). This is a promise of God—a promise to cherish. No matter what others say or do, no matter how badly they hurt you or misuse you, The Lord is always there. It is at those times that we should reach out to Him, the Comforter, the Friend, the Bridge over troubled water, the Prince of Peace. Husbands and loved ones let you down and they leave you when you are at your lowest point, or they take you to the lowest point and then leave you—when the trials of life beat upon you. Take comfort in knowing that He will never leave you; I know that He has never left me. My walk with Him is the only way that I could overcome. Now I can tell my story of how I got over!

Yes, the man I loved left me despite his vow to never leave, but through it all, know that God did not let me down. In life, we are allowed to go through some things to gain strength to face the next situation. In Heb. 13:5, the Lord promises that "I will never leave you nor forsake you." Even through the shadow of death, He is with me. Sometimes it has felt like the shadow of death was over me—the doom and darkness of abuse will cast a shadow that seems darker than death. But in those darkest hours, Jesus is right there, stretching forth His hand, waiting for you to grasp it. Jesus said...*I have come that they may have life, and have it more abundantly.* (John

10:7) I am reminded here of the poem "Footprints." When there is only one set of prints in the sand, God is carrying you and me. He is always there, especially when the way is dark and no light can be seen. *For He has rescued us out of the darkness and gloom of Satan's kingdom and brought us into the Kingdom of his dear Son, who bought our freedom with his blood and forgave us all our sins,* (Co. 1:13-14). Therefore, my sisters, be bold, live abundantly, and proclaim vociferously, "The Lord is my helper, I will not be afraid! What can man do to me? (Heb. 13:6).

CHAPTER 16

MY LIFE WOULD CHANGE FOREVER

Therefore, if man be in Christ, he is a new creature: old things are passed away; behold, all things are become new. And all things are of God, who hath reconciled us to Himself... (II Cor. 5: 17, 18).

Let me begin by saying that this is a project that has been weighing heavily on my heart for some time. I knew that there were other women of faith out there who have suffered the same pain as I was suffering; who needed someone to listen to their stories and to not condemn them for the situation they found themselves in. I am in no way taking a stand that is contrary to religious doctrine and belief. I am not encouraging any woman to leave her husband. For the scripture says that "therefore should a man leave his father and mother and cleave to his wife, and the two shall become one flesh (Gen. 2:24). Now I know that all of our stories are different, yet, they are still the same. I know that the church frowns on divorce, yet, it happens in churches all across this country. We cannot bury our heads in the sand and pretend that people of faith just don't get divorced. Some of us grew up in the church and other places of worship; some of us converted; however way we got there, the point is we are there now. I know that when I got married, and you did also, it was forever— until death do us part. The vows were meaningful and sacred, taken before God and witnesses, and we never expected to be in divorce court. But I have been there and I have heard the judge's gavel; heard the pronouncement that seemingly ripped my heart out and separated me from the one person on this earth whom I loved the most, and in some sense, separated me from the Lord. Because of the state of mind I was in, I couldn't serve the Lord freely. The threats, fear and intimidation, the battering and abuse prevented me from attending church as I desired to do.

Christian, Jewish, Muslim and other women in churches and other places of worship the world over struggle with the question of how to handle a violent and abusive situation, with what the Lord requires of wives who are in such situations, and when to get out of these situations. None of the major world religions condone divorce and neither do I. However, it does happen to a large number of people in churches, and other places of worship, and it is to these people that this ministry is directed. Just as alcoholics or drug addicts need recovery programs to reorient into society, divorcees need to recover and to reorient as well.

When a woman has been *Mrs. Somebody* all of her adult life, and she wakes up one day a single woman, it is very difficult for her to adjust to this new status. People look at her differently, her circle of friends decreases and she is not included in social invitations. The family income greatly decreases causing her to rearrange her life and the lives of her children if she has any. If she has never worked, life becomes increasingly more difficult for her. It is at these times that divorcees need help, support and encouragement. They need acceptance and not ostracism; support and not condemnation; strength and not excommunication; love and not laughter. They need to be connected to a power source that helps them to have faith and to show them how to exercise that faith.

My Life Would Change Forever   79

When I was no longer *Mrs. Somebody*, my life changed. There was no support system to draw from. There were no friends calling to encourage me or inviting me home or out to an event. There was no one praying with me or standing in the gap for me, or interceding on my behalf. I had to go it alone. It is painful, first to find yourself alone again, then secondly to lose the support of many of your fellow friends.

In another or previous time and place, I never believed that I would have to beg for food or ask the church for help, but I did. By this time I had been stripped of all dignity and pride. So I asked; some denied my cries and some reached out. It was through the blessings of those who reached out that I was able to step out of the mire and walk on the green grass beside the still water again.

Recovering after divorce is very difficult. Dealing with the stigma and the shame can be devastating. Restoring yourself in society can also be painstaking. Being left with enormous debt limits your ability to make purchases of the basics of life—food, medicine, and health insurance. A barrage of creditors pursuing you can be overwhelming. If fellow believers with expertise in some of the areas that divorcees face would lend that expertise to the divorcee's recovery, the burden would be so much lighter.

My life changed after divorce and there was a disconnection, sometimes from the power source, sometimes from fellow believers, and sometimes from friends. It seems that when the marital relationship is severed, all other relationships are either severed or damaged. As a divorcee, I am trying to mend my broken heart and renew that relationship with God; I'm trying to reconnect with him and with my fellow believers. If I can help another woman who finds herself in the same life situation, then I have fulfilled the ministry designed for me. Recovery and restoration are important to the health and well-being of anyone who suffers a major loss or lifestyle change such as divorce. Help and support are key ingredients in the recovery process.

Society in general, casts women into certain roles and stigmatizes them in so many ways. On job applications, credit applications, contracts and many other documents there is a category for Married, Widowed, Divorced; Mr. Mrs., Ms. What does it matter? Does being divorced make one credit worthy or a credit risk? In some cases, it is after divorce that women become solvent. During the marriage, she may have had to carry all of the family's financial burdens and may have had difficulty making the ends meet no matter how great the struggle. She may have been forced to step back and to push her husband to be the man that he was created and ordained to be.

If your electricity has ever been off or if you have even had to be in a shelter, or beg for food from relatives, then you can understand what this means. There is a saying that unless you can walk a mile in a man's (woman's) shoes, you cannot understand the roughness of the journey. If you have never had holes in your shoes, then you cannot understand what it means to have your feet soaked in a rain storm as you trudged from store to store with your coupons trying to find bargains to feed your hungry children, and your shoes were padded with newspaper that you borrowed from your neighbor. If you have never had to demean yourself by working on a terrible job that did not pay you nearly enough, yet, you kept the job because it paid some bills and put some food on your

My Life Would Change Forever 81

table, then you cannot understand what the rough side of the mountain is like.

You have to go through the valley in order to appreciate the blessing that is on the other side. Yea though we may walk through the valley, we must fear no evil, for He is with us (Ps. 23). Sometimes He is carrying, not just leading us through the valley.

For some, getting through that valley is the most difficult journey they have ever had to make. You see, some women were stay-at-home moms who raised the children and kept the house; who had dinner ready when husband arrived home from work. At the end of the day she scarcely had time for manicures and new hairstyles, thinking that she could do it on the weekend. And she did when she could. When the announcement or pronouncement came that he was leaving because he no longer found her attractive or that he had fallen in love with someone else, her life, as mine, changed forever. Ten years in the house with three children may not have prepared the housewife for employment, but suddenly she is faced with working outside of the home. What a challenge! It is that rough side of the mountain.

Such women can be victorious by transferring those home management skills into work management skills through networking and communicating, researching and studying. Again, God says that above all things His wish for us is that we prosper. He will make a way.

Your new life will, as my new life did, require some redefining, rearranging and readjusting. Yes, it did change forever. I am no longer the shy, timid, frightened individual who was afraid of holding my head up and looking another person in the eye for fear the oppressor would know it and I would encounter his wrath as a result. Just as I am not the same, neither will you be the same again. Press for the mark of the high calling and run the race with patience, remembering that the race is not given to the swift, nor is it given to the strong, but she who endures to the end will gain the prize. That prize is a new life in Him who is the life-giver.

Praise God from whom all blessings flow!

CHAPTER 17

NOW I'M FREE

O sing unto the Lord a new song;
for he hath done marvelous things...
Let the floods clap their hands:
let the hills be joyful together (Ps. 98:1, 8).

...To worship You like I want to; to pray when
I want to; to sing, to clap my hands, to praise You,
Lord. I can beat my tambourine, clap my cymbals,
and praise you with the loud cymbals! The yoke of
oppression, abuse, degradation, restriction, indignity
and shame is finally broken. Now when I fall down
on my knees my prayers don't have to be hurried.
I'm not concerned about someone walking into my
"secret closet" discovering me and beating, slapping,
kicking me up off my knees. I am free to sing unto
You a new song; to clap my hands, to praise You.
There was a time when I could not because there was
a yoke of oppression around my neck. When there is
a yoke around the neck of Oxen, their movement is
restricted and one ox can't go anywhere without the
other. They are either hitched to a wagon to pull it
along or they must plow the same rows of the field
at the same time. They are in other words bound,
harnessed, conjoined, subject to the desires, direction
and control of the farmer. A yoke may be all right
for an animal that needs to be controlled in order to
accomplish the work of the farm, but a woman's neck
was not made for a yoke.

King Solomon said the woman's (his beloved)
neck is as a tower of ivory or the tower that David
built (Ch 3:4; 4:4). In ivory there is strength and

84 *When The Invitations Stopped*

endurance. Is that the reason Solomon likened the neck to a tower? David built the tower as an armory, whereupon to hang bucklers and shields, a strong place to support the weapons of war. Woman's neck should support the husband who leans on her in a time of despair or when he needs comforting; when her children need soothing, and when her friends cry. It is not to be trampled, or bound and yoked. God gave man dominion over all of the animals, but when He brought the woman to the man at creation, she was given as a helpmeet and not as a slave or a yokel to be bound and oppressed.

Some years ago when I was in bondage, and especially during those years when I thought that I was being a good wife by suffering the abuse (even though I didn't know at the time that it was abuse) and wearing the chains of serfdom, my sister drove over 600 miles from another state three times to free me. Each time I felt like it was my Christian duty to remain; to try a little harder. I believed the promises to do better. I accepted the apologies and the pleadings for forgiveness because I desperately wanted to be loved and accepted. When some small gesture of kindness and pretended love was offered to me, I basked in it, enshrouded myself in it until the cycle repeated itself as it always did and as is always the case with a batterer. Each time she drove away empty and full of despair.

Little did I know that my family and friends hurt as much as I hurt because they loved me and could see a lot more clearly than I could. Yet, they couldn't set me free. They could cry with me and offer me emotional support, but they just could not free me. My sister asked me once if I were going to stay until "*he kills you?*" My closest friends tried to help me—

Now I'm Free

85

to free me, but as the songwriter says, it was only "in God's own time that He set me free."

It was the Saturday before Easter—the holiest of Christian holidays—that I was awakened around 6:30 a.m. after his having been out or up all night, with a demand for intimacy. There had been no intimacy between us for the previous two and one half years. The pattern during these years was to stay out or up all night until I rose from bed to get ready for work, and then he would retire to the bed to sleep during the day while I was at work. Not knowing but suspecting what had been happening during those years because of the changed pattern of behavior and the time spent away from home, I refused. My denial led to pressure, and in a weakened and fearful state, I submitted. Once the act began, it was not loving and tender, but brutal and forceful. I heard the Lord's voice speaking to me saying, **"Enough is enough. You don't have to take this!"**

Immediately and instantly, my 22 years of fear was gone even though I was in an inferior and vulnerable position. For years I had longed to hear the Lord's voice. I prayed to hear it. I listened to hear it. I yearned to hear it. So often I had heard people talk about how the Lord spoke to them and that they could hear His voice just as clearly as they could hear the voice of the person to whom they were speaking. That had not been my experience and it made me question my spirituality because I was neither hearing that clear voice, nor was I hearing that still small voice. I did not know what it sounded like, but that morning at 6:30 a.m. I heard it clearly. **ENOUGH IS ENOUGH!**

At that very moment for the first time in many years, I felt relief and not fear; I had courage and not intimidation—courage to speak the words that were on my heart; the words that got stuck in my throat

86   *When The Invitations Stopped*

so many times; the words to say you will not abuse me anymore; the courage to come in out of the storm that I had been in far too long!

Joe Legunn sings a song with Aretha Franklin entitled "I've Been in the Storm too Long." In the song he says "I need a little time to pray." Someone gave me a tape with that song on it and I played it until it wore out because I felt like I was in a storm, being tossed about by the winds of strife, battered by the hurricanes and splintered by the tornadoes of entrapment and enslavement.

Some of you may be bound by the circumstances of your life. It may be abuse or drugs or some other entrapment that has you bound, but there is a way out. The Gospel songstress, Helen Baylor, was once bound and she sings about it in her story song. When she prayed as I prayed, Jesus, please deliver me from this yoke that is choking my life away, and she rebuked the devil long enough, it was like God Himself said to her as he said to me, **"ENOUGH IS ENOUGH!"** Instantly, she was set free as I was.

I have been delivered! My time has come. Now I am free! The yoke of oppression, abuse, degradation, restriction, indignity and shame is finally broken. Now when I fall down on my knees my prayers don't have to be hurried. I'm not concerned about someone walking into my "secret closet" discovering me and beating, slapping, kicking me up off my knees. I can openly pray before I leave home and not silently mumble a few words to the Lord. I've been set free!

In the days prior to my deliverance I was considered a chattel—a piece of property. I "belonged." About every six months I was accompanied to church not because of a spiritual blessing or for uplifting experience or renewal, but so that the congregation could see "who I belonged to".

Now I'm Free 87

Not only am I physically free, I am also free from the yoke that bound me to an unhealthy and an unhappy situation. I am free from the threats, the intimidation, the emotional battering, the fear, the shame and the pain. I am free from the stares and the questions. I'm free from the painstaking days and the agonizing sleepless nights listening for the key in the lock, fearing and anticipating what would follow. I'm free from the circuitous trips to nowhere that eventually led back to my own driveway. I can take off my girdle and my hose in 90 degree weather. I can cut my hair, or straighten my hair, or style my hair. I no longer have to hide the new dress or new shoes in the closet for 6 months before I can wear them. I'm free!

When the Israelites were in bondage and were asked to sing the songs of Zion, they asked "How can we sing the Lord's song in a strange land?" When I was bound, I couldn't sing or praise the Lord either. But now I can rejoice and sing, making a loud noise. I can praise Him with the voice of rejoicing. Ps. 98 states the floods clap their hands and the hills are joyful together. I can beat my tambourine, clap my cymbals and praise the Lord with the high sounding cymbals because just as the hills are joyful I am joyful, and I am free. I am a new person in Christ Jesus.

Let everything that has breath praise the Lord!

CHAPTER 18

WHEN GOD CALLS YOU BY NAME...

To him the porter openeth; and the sheep hear his voice; and he calls his own sheep by name, and leadeth them out. And when he pulleth forth his own sheep, he goeth before them, and the sheep follow him: for they know his voice (John 10:3, 4).

"...And the sheep hear his voice; and he calleth his own sheep by name...and the sheep follow him; for they know his voice." (John 10:3, 4). He calls all of his children by name—not based on marital status, social standing or level of education, but in dutiful service to Him. He is calling you for something special. The call is different but recognizable. If your child is playing in a group of ten other children, but calls to you, you recognize your child's voice and you heed the call. It is the same way with the Lord. When He calls you, His voice is recognizable and you should heed the call. The Lord doesn't *just* call, when God whispers your name He calls you into action and you must move. He has something special in store for you. Just as He has work for others, He has work for the divorcee to do.

In the middle of our storms we must be able to hear that still, small voice as Jonah did, that calls us by name to newness of life, newness of purpose, and newness of conviction. When God whispers your name, He is calling you into action. He calls all of His children by name. When He whispers your name, He is calling you from the depths of despair, sorrow, and self-pity. He is there waiting to calm the raging storm and to give you peace. Do not get so stuck in the storm that long after the winds and the rains have abated and are no longer raging, you're still hiding. You're hiding behind the cloak of shame, degradation, fear, depression, despondency and grief, knowing that he has taken the best years of your life; that he took everything you had. Cast off all the weights that beset you and open the window of your life and unleash that wrath. Proclaim the promises of God to supply your needs, to wipe away all your tears and to heal your broken heart.

As divorced sisters, we all have experienced, even endured, the pain of knowing that the man we expected to be with forever, no longer wants to be with us. I was married to a man with whom I expected to spend the rest of my life. Well, after 22 years, three months and 17 days, that marriage ended. The devastation was overwhelming. The realization that love no longer existed in the person of a husband flooded every fiber of my being with grief and pain. There were times when I cried all day and all night. At a moment when I least expected it, the tears would overflow as if the Red Sea was raging inside of me. The storms raged and the winds blew. Then, one day God whispered my name, and said, "Move; stop sitting up all night, dry your tears." He called me to newness of life. Not only did He call me, He gave me the zeal to tell my story, to help other women, to encourage other women, and to let them know they are not alone. The first time I told my story I was overcome with tears, reliving the pain and the mental anguish. The audience was composed of medical students preparing to be doctors. In the midst of the tears, God whispered my name as well as many names of people in the audience. Someone was moved to stop the violence and abuse in her life. It was, indeed, moving and deeply emotional for the entire audience. When He whispered my name, I moved. I had grown weary enough.

When He said to me 'enough is enough,' it was clear. I moved on to a new life! In my stormy season, He was my calm, and He will be your calm. I challenge you to try God. He is able and willing, and He will do what He said He would do. He told the lame man to take up his bed and walk and the man who had been crippled from birth walked. He told Naaman to go dip himself in the pool seven times and he would be healed. He told the fishermen to cast their nets on the right side of the boat and they would catch fish. With each command God delivered just what he promised. So when He calls your name and gives you the command, He is ready to deliver you. Move as you have never moved before. He wants to revive you, to renew your spirit, and to set you free. He is a God of action, and so must you be.

Samuel was just a young boy when God called him into His service. The lad had not previously heard the voice of the Almighty, and therefore could not discern whether it was Eli as it called to him while he lay sleeping. When he told the priest, Eli, about the callings, the priest instructed him about how to respond. Now knowing how to discern the voice of God, Samuel waited for the call, and when it came he was ready to respond. Like Samuel, we must train our ears to hear God's voice, because He will call your name and be right on time because He is a God of time. Samuel then listened carefully for the call and when he heard it again, he had the perfect response.

Yes, the storms will rage, the billows will toss and it may seem that God does not care. But even in the raging storm, listen to hear Him whisper your name, and then say as the lad Samuel said at the instruction of Eli, "Speak, Lord, for thy servant hears!" (I Sam. 3:10).

CHAPTER 19

REFLECTIONS

So that we may boldly say, The Lord is my helper, and I will not fear what man shall do unto me (Heb. 13:6).

Love died for us and we wondered why. When we could not figure it out, we cried. We cried for the pain, for the death, for the emptiness in our hearts. We even asked God and our friends and loved ones what we should do. Friends may have offered suggestions and we may have tried many different mechanisms to help us cope, realizing, or at least thinking that the man to whom we were enjoined took everything we had. Some of us went through all five stages of the grieving process as described in Chapter Five, and for some maybe one or two of the stages enabled you to survive and move on. We realized that life does go on—he moved on, probably a lot sooner than you think.

Some fellow believers may have condemned us and ostracized us, and caused us to feel like we did not belong or we did not fit in anymore. However painful this was, we know that if we walk according to the Spirit of the Living God, there is no condemnation. For the law of the Spirit of life has made us free.

I don't know about you, but I tried as hard as I could, endured as much as I could and then some. I feared my children would hate me, and they did hate the situation. However, as they matured and were able to assess the home situation, that hatred turned

94 *When The Invitations Stopped*

to love and admiration for the strength and the will to make it.

I have been loosed from the infirmities that have kept me bound and broken. The issue of blood has been resolved and God has spoken to womanhood and has given you and me, the new woman, a voice. Just as I am doing, you are to let your voice be heard. Sing praises to Him for the spirit of forgiveness—for being able to forgive; for wanting to forgive; for the peace that results from forgiving; for forgiving yourself and everyone else that you think has wronged you. It is in and through forgiving that the countenance can be illumined and the light of God's love can shine through.

Yes, some invitations stopped and we have had many meals at a table for one. We missed seeing some plays or some concerts. We missed some baseball, basketball, or football games and tailgate parties because no one invited us, but we changed the rules and tricked society. Who cares how you butter your bread? The important thing is that you have bread— pita, wheat, rye, pumpernickel, or cornbread—and you can buy it at the deli and butter it however way you like at your *Table for One, Please!*

Now you are strong and self-confident. You are reconnected to the heavenly pipeline—going back to school, having a system of support, singing your song, playing your part—because now you know that you are worthy. How do you know? You know because God says you are worthy, and if He says so, believe it! He is a God who cannot lie and no matter what the circumstances, He will never leave you or abandon you. Just turn to Him, call on Him. When friends and loved ones let you down and husbands tear you down,

Reflections

and the cares of life weigh you down, He says, "I will never leave you nor forsake you." Rejoice, I say!

Yes, life changes and takes detours. Change allows us to unlock and unleash our full potential, to develop talents that have been dormant; to fulfill dreams—to even dream. Change brings freedom from abuse, oppression, depression, degradation, intimidation and humiliation. Change brings freedom to worship, to serve, to assist, to be assisted. Change allows for a connection with others outside of your little world. Change knocks down walls and barriers that have separated you and kept you bound so that you thought that what was happening to you was normal—that all married people go through it. Now you know that it is not normal and no one has the right to abuse you. Help is available. The laying on of hands is reserved and sanctified for the men and women of God in the anointing of saints, not by angry husbands and others in fits of rage.

We are free to praise, to thank, to shout, to bless, to live the abundant life. We are free to invite and be invited. We are free to help and to be helped, to speak and to be heard because God has called each one of us by name. We have heard His voice and are following His lead. Therefore, if you are in God, you are a new creature: Old things are passed away (I Cor. 5:17). Have hope, for God's compassions fail not. They are new every morning. Great is thy faithfulness!

CHAPTER 20

RESOURCES

If you are in an abusive relationship and you choose to remain, there are some tips to help you. Remember, I stated in the beginning that I am not advocating that any woman leave her husband. That is a choice that only you can make. I would prefer that all marriages would survive and that couples would be together for life. The following tips for women staying in abusive relationships may be helpful to you:

1. Remember that you have the right to live without fear and violence.
2. You deserve NOT to be abused regardless of what you may have done.
3. Do not blame yourself for the violence. The abuser is the one committing the crime. Remember that **DOMESTIC VIOLENCE IS A CRIME!**
4. Know that you are not alone with this problem, but use and trust your support systems.
5. Be honest with your children. They are already aware of what is going on even if they do not talk about it.
6. Learn about available resources, and become educated about the issues of domestic violence.
7. Be honest with yourself, and don't "play down" the abuse. Don't make excuses for the abuser.
8. Get involved with self-improvement programs that appropriately meet your needs.
9. Take steps to establish your own existence to eliminate control by anyone.
10. Develop a "plan of action" for a life without your

mate if you decide to leave the relationship.

11. Don't feel guilty for making plans to take care of yourself and your children.
12. Do what you have to do to keep you and your children safe.
13. Keep your mind and body healthy, and do something nice for yourself on a daily basis.

DEVELOP A SAFETY PLAN

- Dial 911 if you are ever in danger.
- Have extra car keys made.
- Develop danger signals or codes for your family, children, and neighbors.
- Identify dangerous locations in the house and try to avoid being trapped in these rooms.
- Practice escape routes in your mind.
- Make plans in advance for a safe place to go.
- Have extra money hidden in a safe place if you leave.
- Have bank account, credit and ATM cards, and savings passbooks information.
- Have phone numbers and addresses for family and friends available.
- Assemble important papers, birth certificates, marriage license, social security numbers for you and your children, school and health records, medications and prescriptions, insurance papers, financial, etc. KEEP THESE ITEMS IN A SAFE PLACE!

IMPORTANT NATIONAL TOLL-FREE NUMBERS

These numbers are not for reporting child abuse. These numbers offer support, counseling, referrals, or information. Be sure to clarify what you are looking for and ask what they provide when you call.

Family Violence Prevention Fund/Health Resource Center
(800) 313-1310

National Domestic Violence Hotline
(800) 799-7233

National Resource Center on Domestic Violence
(800) 537-2238

Rape, Abuse & Incest National Network
(800) 656-4673

Resource Center on Domestic Violence, Child Protection and Custody
(800) 527-3223

National Parent Information Network
(800) 583-4135

Single Parents Association
(800) 704-2102

Gerber Information Line
(800) 443-7237

HOW TO HELP A BATTERED WOMAN

There are many who would like to help battered women, but they don't know how. Noted below are some answers to many of the questions individuals ask about what to do or say when wanting to assist someone who may be in an abusive relationship. Almost everyone knows or will meet a woman who is being abused. Here are some ideas to help victims in one-on-one situations.

1. Believe her story.
2. Listen and give non-blaming feedback.
3. Let her know she is not alone.
4. Let her know that her's is not the only relationship in which violence occurs. At least one out of every five women in this country will experience partner abuse.
5. Realize the severity and danger of abuse and domestic violence. Fifty percent (50%) of women in abusive relationships are killed.
6. Let her know that she is not to blame and she is not responsible for HIS abusive behavior. He CHOSE to abuse her.
7. Let her know that the assault is a crime ... the same as if a stranger assaults her.
8. Do not assume she knows her rights, resources and options.
9. Don't offer advice. Offer her support for her choices.
10. Help her to realize her strengths.
11. Help her to see how his violence has changed her behavior and life.
12. Be non-judgmental; be aware of your own experiences and attitudes.

102 *When The Invitations Stopped*

13. Be realistic about your time, energy limitations, and what you can give.
14. Let her know that she can talk to you again.

Remember, the victim should be encouraged to express anger and will need support to avoid feeling overwhelmed by her anger. It is important to let her know that you don't think that the myths about her are true. Learning to make decisions is an important first step for the battered woman to regain control of her existence.

We'd love to have you download our catalog of
titles we publish at:

www.TEACHServices.com

or write or email us your thoughts,
reactions, or criticism about this
or any other book we publish at:

TEACH Services, Inc.
254 Donovan Road
Brushton, NY 12916

info@TEACHServices.com

or you may call us at:

518/358-3494